Ada's Algorithm
the Ada Lovelace musical

a new two-act musical

Libretto and lyrics by James Essinger

Additional material by Mo Pietroni-Spenst

Ada's Algorithm - the Ada Lovelace musical

Published by The Conrad Press in the United Kingdom 2020

Tel: +44(0)1227 472 874
www.theconradpress.com
info@theconradpress.com

ISBN 978-1-913567-14-9

Typesetting and Cover Design by: Charlotte Mouncey, www.bookstyle.co.uk
The Conrad Press logo was designed by Maria Priestley.

Printed and bound in Great Britain by Clays Ltd, Elcograf S.p.A.

Ada's Algorithm

the Ada Lovelace musical

a new two-act musical

libretto and lyrics by James Essinger
music by Philip Henderson,
Jenni Pinnock and James Taylor

additional material by
Mo Pietroni-Spenst and Philip Henderson

This libretto is dedicated to the memory of Fritz Löhner-Beda, librettist, whose works include *Das Land des Lächelns* (*'The Land of Smiles'*) born June 24 1883, murdered by the Nazis in Monowitz concentration camp, December 4 1942.

Photograph by Karl Winkler

Preface

I've been professionally more or less obsessed with Ada Lovelace (1815-1852) since the late 1990s, when I became interested in her while studying the life and work of Victorian mathematician Charles Babbage.

A biography I wrote of Ada, *Ada's Algorithm*, was published in the UK in 2013 and in the US in 2014. Spanish-language and Finnish-language editions have also been published, and a movie option on the book sold to Monumental Pictures. This has all been gratifying; I wrote the biography in the winter of 2011-2012 for a tiny advance and without any expectation that the book would find a fairly large readership.

I'm not sure when exactly the idea of writing a musical about Ada came to me, but I've certainly been thinking about it since about 2013, which was when I was fortunate enough to meet a Canterbury-based composer, Ethan Lewis Maltby and also a performing arts teacher and researcher, Mo Pietroni, who became Mo Pietroni-Spenst in 2014.

I was keen to try to get to know a composer: a profession I've always held in great awe, despite, perhaps, Sir Tim Rice's comment in his riveting autobiography *Oh, What a Circus* (2012). Sir Tim argues that composers have it easier than lyricists, as composers can usually think of a tune pretty quickly, whereas writing lyrics is hard work. When I met Ethan and Mo, I had no belief in my ability to write either a libretto or lyrics, whether through hard work or not.

At that time, I hadn't worked out the plot of a possible Ada musical in any detail. After meeting Ethan and Mo, though, and being impressed by their talent, and influenced as I was by knowing from the research for the biography that Ada had lived in a house called Bifrons, near Canterbury, when she was twelve years old, I suggested we should start with a song about Ada meeting some village children in the Kentish countryside. The idea was that Ada was doing her best to make friends with them. Ethan and Mo liked the idea, so I asked them to work together on the song. I was happy about that, as I was working on several other projects, including a new biography about the friendship of Charles Babbage and Ada, and I still thought of the Ada musical idea as something fairly tangential to everything else I was doing.

I heard nothing from Ethan or Mo for some weeks, but then was delighted when they told me they'd composed a song, 'Little Miss High and Mighty', with music by Ethan and lyrics by Mo.

I loved the song. It has become extremely, and deservedly, successful on YouTube, where a wonderful performance of it by Spirit Young Performers currently (as of May 2020) has more than three million views.

After this, nothing much happened with the musical for a few years. I was still convinced that writing a libretto, let alone song lyrics, was beyond me. Even though I had had fiction and non-fiction published on both sides of the Atlantic, I still didn't have any confidence I could write the script for a musical, let alone the words for songs. But I didn't see how I could write song lyrics unless I knew what the music was, nor did I see how I could know *that* unless there were some words first.

I should have known better, because I'd been a fan of Gilbert and Sullivan ever since seeing a wonderful performance of *The Mikado* at the White Rock Theatre in Hastings, southern

England, in 1986. I already knew that W.S. Gilbert had written all the songs as well as the script, before Sir Arthur Sullivan set the songs to music. Yet I still uncharacteristically procrastinated, and even commissioned a completely new person to write a libretto of the musical. But that person gave up after drafting about a dozen pages, and I didn't like her material at all.

So, finally, in January 2017, I decided that unless I had a go at writing the libretto for the musical myself and the lyrics for the remaining songs too - I wanted to incorporate 'Little Miss High and Mighty' into the script and also some other excellent material Mo had written – the Ada musical might never exist.

So I set to work. I felt strangely privileged to be writing an entire musical in which 'Little Miss High and Mighty' could slot. By this point that song had been around, a kind of orphan without a parent musical, for at least three years, though it was already building up a fan base on YouTube. I suppose at this point the song was rather like that wonderful 1967 track 'Grocer Jack', which was designed to be part of a work called *A Teenage Opera*. The overall work was originally completed but is nowhere near as popular as 'Grocer Jack', which was a deserved huge hit in several countries.

I couldn't think how to write lyrics other than to compose the individual songs as poems and with some kind of rhythm in my head. I can't compose music at all and while I love singing I have no talent for playing a musical instrument. I played the violin very badly at school and gave it up when I failed Grade Two, seven years after starting. I never managed to master third position; I never even got the hang of where to put my fingers for first position, and I still don't understand why violins aren't built with frets.

But I'm sensitive to and susceptible to music, as most of us are, I suppose, and sometimes I wrote the lyrics by thinking of a song I liked, using the rhythm of the song and then discarding the rhythm so the lyrics stood by themselves, or so I hoped.

I wrote most of the libretto and lyrics late in the evening after working at my day job: writing fiction and non-fiction and also running a publishing firm called The Conrad Press, which I set up in December 2015. Because I was writing the songs often quite late at night, their rhythms and words stuck in my mind and it was difficult to forget about them during the day. This was not something I had anticipated. Sir Tim is right: writing lyrics is hard work.

The actual writing of the libretto and lyrics took me about three months altogether. For much of that time I was weirdly affected by the rhythm of the songs, especially as I was going to bed far too late: nowadays I no longer work until the early hours of the morning as I used to do in those days: you get a lot done but your health suffers.

I've always felt that musical theatre is an incredibly exciting art form and that a great musical theatre experience is, arguably, the best kind of experience one can have in the theatre. This is because, if it all works well, then the audience gets to enjoy drama, spectacle, dialogue, dancing, excitement and the delight of all of this is enhanced by the music.

Personally, my favourite musicals are *The Land of Smiles*, *Fiddler on the Roof*, *Oklahoma*, *The Mikado*, *The Pirates of Penzance*, *HMS Pinafore* and the three Andrew Lloyd Webber and Tim Rice masterpieces: *Joseph and the Amazing Technicolor Dreamcoat*, *Jesus Christ Superstar* and *Evita*. Indeed, the enormous narrative power of *Evita* was a contributing factor in my belief that a musical about Ada was worth writing. There are many similarities between the life of Ada Lovelace and the life of Eva Peron. Both women died much too young and of a tragic disease, and both were, in a sense, failures in their lifetime who have had, and surely will continue to have in the future, an extremely powerful lasting effect as iconic heroines, even though they came from very different times and backgrounds.

My favourite musical of all, *The Land of Smiles*, (*Das Land des Lächelns* in German) was premiered on October 10 1929 at the Metropol Theatre in Berlin. My late father Ted, born in Germany in 1922, loved the musical and used to play it a great deal at our home in Leicester in the 1960s and 1970s.

While perhaps *The Land of Smiles* is not objectively a truly great musical - it is somewhat melodramatic and the emotions it generates could fairly be said to be rather stylised - in all fairness it was written as an operetta and before the modern musical, with its emphasis on naturalism and realism, was properly invented. *The Land of Smiles* has, in fact, many moments of sheer genius in the libretto and lyrics by Fritz Löhner-Beda and consistantly wonderful tunes from the composer Franz Lehar. I plan before long, all being well, to write a modern translation, into English, of the libretto and lyrics.

While I was working on *Ada's Algorithm - the Ada Lovelace musical* I was appalled to discover that Fritz Löhner-Beda was murdered at the age of fifty-nine by the Nazis on December 4 1942. Lehar, who knew Hitler, tried unsuccessfully to have Löhner-Beda released from Monowitz camp without success: the great lyricist's Jewishness overrode, in the warped, evil, minds of the Nazis, all that he had bestowed upon the German language and the abundance of joy he had given audiences.

I dedicate this libretto to Fritz Löhner-Beda. If imitation is indeed the most sincere form of flattery, I am proud that two songs in the Ada musical - 'A Dream of Tom' and 'Forever Loving Friends' - have melodies and emotional ideas based on two songs from *The Land of Smiles*. I freely acknowledge these borrowings in the libretto.

What happens now to *Ada's Algorithm - the Ada Lovelace musical* remains to be seen. I believe that the songs, due to the great talent of the composers, are emotionally engaging, beautifully tuneful, and wide-ranging in their scope and tone, from the first scene-setting song, 'The glorious Industrial Revolution' to lovely arias such as 'As a woman I was doomed from the start', to memorable duets such as 'The wonders of machinery', and a host of splendid melodies such as 'When a man says he love you, don't believe him!' and the lullaby, 'I walk across the mystic line that shadows life and death' and Babbage's 'May I never fall prey to irrational emotion' and many others.

At the time of writing there has not yet been a performance of *Ada's Algorithm - the Ada Lovelace musical*. While I accept that publishing a musical's libretto and lyrics before it has been established in the canon of musicals is somewhat unusual, it seems a sensible idea to give readers the opportunity to decide what they think of this new musical.

Certainly, Ada's remarkable and tragic life was packed with drama and inspiration. The truth is that even the genius Charles Babbage did not have the perception that his cogwheel computer - which he called the Analytical Engine and never completed in his lifetime, nor has it yet been completed since - could be used for all sorts of purposes other than simple mathematical calculations.

Ada, on the other hand, did see this. Her brilliant and utterly inspired vision of what a computer could be makes her one of the most important women in the history of science.

Today, as Lord Byron's Ghost tells us at the end of the musical, Ada is indeed '... *seen as a crusader/For understanding, better than Babbage, the potential of the computer,/Today a billion Ada fans eternally salute her!*'

Finally, and I am mentioning this here partly because it will make the mutually contemptuous song from The Analytical Engine and The Difference Engine easier to understand, I should point out that a full-size working calculating section of Babbage's design for his Difference Engine was successfully built in 1991. The printing mechanism was completed in 2002.

The builds were engineered by a team from the London Science Museum, under the leadership of Doron Swade, then Curator of Computing. This modern project to construct a Difference Engine was carefully organised using only materials, and levels of precision, that would have been available to Babbage himself. The success of the project proved that Babbage was right: the Difference Engine would have worked and very likely the Analytic Engine would have worked too.

James Essinger May 2020

Ada's Algorithm
the Ada Lovelace Musical

Musical Numbers

ACT ONE

1 - THE GLORIOUS INDUSTRIAL REVOLUTION

2 - THE ARGUMENT

3 - SITTING ALONE, LOOKING UP AT THE SKY

4 - IS THY FACE LIKE THY MOTHER'S, MY FAIR CHILD?

5 - LITTLE MISS HIGH AND MIGHTY

6 - THE WONDERS OF MACHINERY

7 - HEARTS HURT AND ACHE

8 - OH, TOM, MY LOVE!

9 - THE WONDERS OF MACHINERY (REPRISE)

10 - WHEN A MAN SAYS HE LOVES YOU, DON'T BELIEVE HIM!

11 - THE JACQUARD LOOM

12 - WHAT AN AMAZING IDEA – A COMPUTER!

13 - SUNKEN ROCKS AT SEA

14 - A DREAM OF TOM

15 - OH FUTURE DWELLERS, WHEN YOU THINK OF ME

16 - HE'S NOT THE ONE SHE REALLY WANTS!

ACT TWO

1 - SO MAYBE YOU THINK ADA'S MARRIAGE WILL TAME HER?

2 - MAY I NEVER FALL PREY TO IRRATIONAL EMOTION

3 - FOREVER LOVING FRIENDS

4 - THE LULLABY

5 - MY MIND IS FULLY OPEN TO YOUR LUDICROUS INVENTION

6 - OH, I'M POSITIVELY ANALYTICAL

7 - AS A WOMAN I WAS DOOMED FROM THE START

8 - I'M LYING HERE SADLY WATCHING THE SKY

9 - 1st Finale: OH, TOM, MY LOVE! (REPRISE)

10 - 2nd Finale: WE'VE SEEN ALL OUR DREAMS COME TRUE

Scenes

ACT ONE

ACT TWO

Principal characters

Ada Byron (later Ada Lovelace)
Lady Byron
Lord Byron's Ghost
Tom Newton (later Sir Thomas Newton)
Charles Babbage
Bob Peel (later Sir Robert Peel)

Supporting characters

Miss Lucas
Walker, Lady Byron's butler
Lady Broadstairs
The Viscount of Whitstable
The Duke of Derbyshire
Lord Lovelace
Lord Worthing
Reverend Cusworth
Edward Simmonds

Child characters

Georgie Babbage - Babbage's daughter,
(born July 17 1818 so three years younger than Ada)
Briggsy, 16 - the butcher's boy
George, 15 - a rough village boy
Ethel, 15 - George's girlfriend
Byron Lovelace, 6 - one of Ada's two sons
Annabella Lovelace, 5 - Ada's daughter

ACT ONE

SCENE 1 - A LONDON STREET. JUNE 1831

SONG - THE GLORIOUS
INDUSTRIAL REVOLUTION

ADA BYRON sixteen years old, runs onto the stage

ADA: Neolithic days have fortunately fled
When hunters all used flints and spears to keep their
family fed.

BOB PEEL, also sixteen, runs onto the stage.

BOB: And in the Dark Ages, which were a lot more recent
You had to use an iron sword to live halfway decent.

ADA: These lamentable precursors to today's hi-tech solutions
Never once involved transformational revolutions,

BOB: Not the kind of revolution that overthrows a king
But one applying practical science to
almost everything!

ADA: That useful device, the sewing machine
Use a foot treadle to sew!

BOB: Sparks flowing in a well-ordered stream,
The miracle of the electric dynamo!

ADA: The mackintosh, which wards off rain
And quickly makes you dry again!

BOB: The ending of linguistic tiffs
By decryption of the hieroglyphs!

ADA:　　　　　　　Blurred and woolly thinking has finally gone
　　　　　　　　　In this revolutionary year, 1831!

ADA and BOB:　　For many tasks we now have ingenious appliances
　　　　　　　　　Conjured from the miracles of the practical sciences!

BOB:　　　　　　 *(suddenly in a provocative sexist way)*
　　　　　　　　　And the people who conjure these miracles are men,
　　　　　　　　　We chaps have shown ourselves to be supreme
　　　　　　　　　yet again,
　　　　　　　　　Inventors' studios are in no way swimmin'
　　　　　　　　　With opportunities for argumentative women.
　　　　　　　　　There's no room for female emotional scenes
　　　　　　　　　In offices where men design wondrous machines.
　　　　　　　　　Women enjoy flowers, make-up and dresses,
　　　　　　　　　But none of these are wanted at scientific addresses.
　　　　　　　　　Of course we love women as girlfriends and wives
　　　　　　　　　But we want them to stay *out* of our scientific lives.
　　　　　　　　　In Britain the Industrial Revolution was unfurled
　　　　　　　　　And London is the centre of this glorious new world!

ADA:　　　　　　 *(fighting back)*
　　　　　　　　　The only reason we don't get a scientific chance
　　　　　　　　　Is because we're stuck at home washing all your shirts
　　　　　　　　　and pants!
　　　　　　　　　'Argumentative'? That's a pretty sick joke
　　　　　　　　　No-one loves a quarrel more than a bloke.
　　　　　　　　　We cater to all your needs, daily and nocturnal
　　　　　　　　　You want us to be girlfriends, cooks, cleaners…
　　　　　　　　　and maternal.
　　　　　　　　　Besides, all your glorious machines don't even work!
　　　　　　　　　If you invent a washing-machine, you'll get a grate-
　　　　　　　　　ful smirk.

> We run your homes, we make your meals, we bring
> your children up
> You were certainly inventive when designing
> that set-up!
> But very soon with your own laundry you will all
> be lumbered
> Because our days of being in your thrall are
> surely numbered!

BOB: *(to ADA)* Ada, I wonder if you happen to be free on Saturday evening? I know an excellent dining-house where they serve first-rate turtle soup, and mutton chops.

ADA: Well, yes, I am free, but I don't want a date with you, thanks.

BOB: But why not? *(indicating himself)* What's not to like?

ADA: I think you'd find me far too argumentative.

Ada and Bob exit by opposite sides.

SCENE 2 - LADY BYRON'S LONDON HOME
JUNE 1831

ADA BYRON'S governess, MISS LUCAS, runs on, followed by Ada's mother LADY BYRON, wringing her hands.

MISS LUCAS: Lady Byron, I can't go on like this!

LADY BYRON: But… you're my last hope!

MISS LUCAS: I'm sorry, but I've had enough.

LADY BYRON: Please, don't make me go through it all again.

MISS LUCAS: I've done my best, but your daughter is *impossible*.

LADY BYRON: That's not true! She may be a little... headstrong –

MISS LUCAS: Headstrong? Is that what you call it? She's a tyrant!

LADY BYRON: She does have a somewhat inventive mind, I admit.

Ada comes on, looking innocent.

LADY BYRON: Ada, where have you been?

ADA: Having an argument in the street with a silly boy.

LADY BYRON: It isn't ladylike to quarrel in the street.

ADA: I had to set him right, Mama!... I'm thinking about how I'm going to change the world by being a great scientist and inventor. There's so much being invented right now, but so much more that hasn't been invented yet!... oh, hello, Miss Lucas.

LADY BYRON: Yes, yes, well, you can start by inventing a way of behaving yourself when you're with your governess! I hear from Miss Lucas you've been impertinent in lessons again and answering back!

ADA: I wasn't answering back! We were studying and I just explained to Miss Lucas that -

MISS LUCAS: I'll do the explaining, thank you very much!

ADA: But you don't even know what a quadratic equation is!

MISS LUCAS: Of course I know what a quadratic equation is!

ADA: What is it then?

MISS LUCAS: It's... well, it's an equation that was invented by a professor who lived in the *quadrangle* of an Oxford college.

ADA: What nonsense! It's an equation having the form 'ax squared plus bx equals c'.

LADY BYRON: Stop showing off! And you must be respectful to Miss Lucas.

ADA: But she had it all wrong, Mama! How am I supposed to learn my lessons when my governess doesn't understand them herself? I may as well get my cat Puff to teach me!

LADY BYRON: Ada, Miss Lucas came with a personal recommendation from the royal family. If she's good enough to have taught the king's nephews and nieces she's good enough for you.

ADA: Well, there's no accounting for taste!

LADY BYRON: Ada! That's enough!

MISS LUCAS: I'm leaving, your Ladyship. I would like my wages please.

LADY BYRON: Oh, Miss Lucas, please stay. I don't want to lose another governess. Poor Ada will be left without anyone to teach her.

MISS LUCAS: She should have thought of that when she said that there are fish swimming about in the River Thames who know more about physics than I do!

LADY BYRON: *(to Ada)* Did you really say that to Miss Lucas?

ADA: I… might have, by accident.

SONG - THE ARGUMENT

ADA, LADY BYRON AND MISS LUCAS

LADY BYRON
What to do? What to do?
I'm at my wits' end over you.
Never a contented child,
Running free and running wild,
Impossible to hold you back -
I think my head might crack!

MISS LUCAS
You're not the only one.
I've never had to work so hard
To keep a child under control.
It's impossible to teach this girl.
I'm doing everything I can,
But this job is destroying my soul!

ADA
You talk about impossible.
I'll tell you what's impossible:
A so-called 'tutor' who needs lessons of her own.
I'd rather study by myself
Than listen to that old crone!

MISS LUCAS
Well I never!

LADY BYRON
Ada, I won't take this anymore!
Keep up this behaviour and just see what lies in store.
Just show your elders some respect.

MISS LUCAS
That's really all that I expect.

ADA
But this is so unfair!
Say what you like, I really don't care.
I know that you are just trying to look strong,
But why should I be punished when Miss Lucas is in the wrong?

MISS LUCAS
That's it! I've had enough!
I'm sorry, Lady Byron –
I've never given up before –
But there's a fact you've got to face:
Ada's a hopeless case!
I can't be her governess,
I can't be her governess no more!

ADA
I think you mean, 'any more'.

MISS LUCAS
You really are the limit, Ada!

MISS LUCAS storms off in a huff.

ADA: Thank goodness she's gone! Mama, I've been thinking lots and lots about my plans to fly. I want to build a steam-horse made of iron and steel with pistons and wheels and great wings like Pegasus and I'll fill it with coal and light the boiler and it'll soar over London and I'll be able to look down and wave at you!

LADY BYRON: Haven't I told you many times to control your imagination? Your father never did and look what happened to him! Your father went mad - or perhaps he was mad all the time, it's perfectly possible. Do you want to be like him? I'm sure you don't.

ADA: But Mama, don't you think my flying-machine a wonderful idea?

LADY BYRON: No, I don't. I think it's a ridiculous and very dangerous notion. If God had meant people to fly, he'd have fitted us with wings instead of arms and legs!

ADA: Mama, you might as well say that if God had meant us to write letters, he'd have fitted us with writing-desks!

LADY BYRON: I'm so weary of your constant interruptions and answering back! Now listen Ada, I've rented a large house, Bifrons, in the countryside near Canterbury in Kent until Michaelmas and we're going to live there next week.

ADA: What if I don't want to go to Kent?

LADY BYRON: Ada, not everything I say is a matter for discussion. This isn't. I hope the fresh country air will bring you to your senses and improve your behaviour. I'll find you a new governess in Canterbury. Oh, and I'll be inviting two good friends of mine, the Viscount of Whitstable and Lady Broadstairs, to dinner at Bifrons before long. You can join us, but I'll expect you to behave yourself.

ADA: There's a whole world out there of inventions just waiting to be thought up, and all you want me to do is make me go to a dinner-party!

LADY BYRON: You need to get your head out of the clouds and put your feet firmly on the ground!

ADA: My feet *are* on the ground! It's getting them off that's the problem!

LADY BYRON: You sound just like your father!

ADA: But he had such a wonderful imagination!

LADY BYRON: I will *not* have you end up like Lord Byron!

ADA: Mama, I love my papa, and I never even met him! And he's dead and I never shall!

LADY BYRON: *(in a moment of affection)* My darling girl, it is better this way! If he were still alive and living in England… he'd ruin your life as he ruined mine!

LADY BYRON exits.

SONG - SITTING ALONE, LOOKING UP AT THE SKY

ADA

Sitting alone, looking up at the sky,
Dreaming of inventions I'd so like to try,
Will I ever be someone great in this world?
Could I be much more this dreamy young girl?

I see machines being invented, such wonders! Oh my!
But it's men who invent them... yet maybe, could I?

Notions explode every day in my head,
There's nothing quite like them in books that I've read.
My thoughts all take shape like pictures in dreams,
Are my glimpses of progress as real as they seem?

I could make a machine that flies through the night,
Millions would cheer me on seeing that sight.
Flying to heaven and even beyond,
Between people and God I'll forge a new bond,
And I, Ada Byron, will be queen of the night,
If you're sitting beside me, best hold on tight!

As my confidence grew, I'd fly in the day,
And King William below would admire me and say
'I thought Ada Byron was winsome and coy,
But no, she's the equal of the cleverest boy!'

I'll show you my steam-horse, made of wood and of steel,
With wings to propel us, we'd have no need for wheels!

Notions explode every day in my head,
There's nothing quite like them in books that I've read.
My thoughts take shape like pictures in dreams,
Are my glimpses of progress as real as they seem?

I see machines invented, such wonders! Oh my!
But it's men who invent them... well, so can I!

SCENE 3 - THE DINING-ROOM AT BIFRONS

The following Saturday evening. Lady Byron and Ada are at the table along with the VISCOUNT OF WHITSTABLE, a thoughtful, alert and distinguished-looking gentleman in handsome dress, and LADY BROADSTAIRS, an over-confident lady blessed more by wealth than brains. Ada is wearing a pretty dress.

LADY BROADSTAIRS: That's a lovely dress, Ada.

LADY BYRON: It is indeed, Lady Broadstairs, and made of the very finest silk.

ADA: I know it's a nice dress, but I do wish Mama hadn't made me wear it.

VISCOUNT OF WHITSTABLE: Why is that, my dear?

ADA: I feel bad about all the poor silkworms!

LADY BYRON: What are you talking about?

ADA: Thousands of them have to be killed to make just one silk dress. Yes, Mama, they use boiling water, which kills all the caterpillars, and then they unravel their little cocoons one by one –

LADY BYRON: *(to Lady Broadstairs and the Viscount)* I'm afraid Ada spends far too much time thinking about things that don't matter.

VISCOUNT OF WHITSTABLE: Oh I consider Ada to have a most interesting mind. I really enjoyed her telling us about her plans for building a steam-powered flying-machine.

LADY BROADSTAIRS: But what if it ran out of coal and crashed to earth! *(to Ada)* What a girl like you needs to think about is how to be charming. The day will come, and not so long in the future either, when you'll have a husband and he'll want you to look nice and be respectful.

ADA: I'll *never* get married… not unless I can find a man who fills me with noble thoughts and is a scientist and inventor, so we can invent things together!

LADY BROADSTAIRS: My dear Lady Byron, I think Ada has a great deal to learn!

VISCOUNT OF WHITSTABLE: Did you know, Ada, that I met your father once, at Cambridge University?

ADA: Oh, please tell me what Papa was like!

VISCOUNT OF WHITSTABLE: A rather boisterous fellow, as I recall, but good-natured. He owned a bear. I remember it used to dance, and was very fond of beer.

LADY BYRON: It had *that* in common with its owner.

ADA: *(to the Viscount)* Do you know Papa wrote a poem about me?

VISCOUNT OF WHITSTABLE: He did?

ADA: Yes. It's beautiful. I know it by heart.

VISCOUNT OF WHITSTABLE: I'd love to hear it.

SONG - IS THY FACE LIKE THY MOTHER'S, MY FAIR CHILD?

ADA

Is thy face like thy mother's, my fair child!
Ada! sole daughter of my house and heart?
When last I saw thy young blue eyes they smiled,
And then we parted, -- not as now we part,
But with a hope. -- Awaking with a start,
The waters heave around me; and on high
The winds lift up their voices: I depart,
Whither I know not; but the hour's gone by,
When Albion's lessening shores could grieve or glad mine eye.

VISCOUNT OF WHITSTABLE: Bravo! ... As for the steam-horse, it sounds to me an excellent idea. I think Ada should be given every encouragement to make the most of her talents. Alas, my late wife and I could not have children. Lady Byron, you are very fortunate to have Ada. Children are a great blessing.

LADY BYRON: Yes, they are, but they can be most troublesome too.

ADA: *(to Lady Byron)* I wish you had let me go and live with Papa in Italy! I might have been able to save his life when he became ill. I would have cared for him.

LADY BYRON: You should be grateful I didn't let you go to join your father there! He would certainly have neglected you, just as he neglected your illegitimate half-sister Allegra. You remember what happened to her: your father sent her to a convent, where she died of fever aged only five.

ADA: Yes, Mama, I know. You've told me about her often enough! I may as well live in a convent myself! I don't have any friends at all!

Ada runs off.

VISCOUNT OF WHITSTABLE: (calling after Ada) Ada, I very much hope your flying-machine gets off the ground!

SCENE 4 - A COUNTRY LANE NEAR BIFRONS

Early the following morning. Ada, in a plainer but still lovely dress, is walking down the lane, carrying a sketch-pad. Three scruffy VILLAGE CHILDREN come on, playing with hoops. These children are BRIGGSY, aged 16, the butcher's boy, a local thug; GEORGE, 15, Briggsy's sidekick and George's girlfriend, ETHEL aged 15. Seeing Ada, the three village children stop playing and come up to her, surrounding Ada as if she were some exotic curiosity.

ETHEL: *(to Ada)* Who are you, then?

ADA: *(cheerfully, could these children be the friends she's looking for?)* I'm Ada Byron.

ETHEL: Where d'you live?

ADA: At Bifrons House. I'm Lady Byron's daughter.

ETHEL: *(pointing to the sketch-pad)* What's that?

ADA: My sketch-pad. I want to draw some birds.

ETHEL: Why?

ADA: So I can learn how their wings work. You see, I want to build a steam-horse and fly through the sky in it.

Ethel just laughs. She turns to Briggsy and George.

ETHEL: She's completely mental!

SONG - LITTLE MISS HIGH AND MIGHTY

BRIGGSY, ETHEL AND GEORGE

BRIGGSY:
Who have we got here?
Looking quite the little lady.

ETHEL:
Do you know the way, my dear?
Cos the woods get dark and shady.

BRIGGSY:
Will you look at 'er posh dress?

ETHEL:
Wouldn't want it to get dirty.

GEORGE:
So chuck her in the mud
Let's see her get all shirty

ETHEL:
You should buy better manners
If you've got so much money.
Cos we get quite offended
When you look at us funny.

35

BRIGGSY: Who d'you think you are?
              S'pose you think you're something special

ETHEL: Well, you're not getting very far
              Now you've met

BRIGGSY: Briggsy,

GEORGE: George

ETHEL: and Ethel

ADA: Leave me alone.

BRIGGSY: No, we might not have the talk

ADA: Please, go away

BRIGGSY: All them gents and ladies do
              But we're a happy bunch

ADA: I don't disagree!

BRIGGSY: Cos we got freedom unlike you

ADA: I have -

ETHEL: You don't know our manners
              Cos you're not from the village

GEORGE: Your eyes move right past us
              When you ride in your carriage

BRIGGSY, GEORGE and ETHEL:
We live so free, a life without money
Don't mean we've got nothing, we have all we need.
Climbing up trees and sliding down hay bales,
The world is our playground.
But you come along, like we're in the wrong
Lit-tle miss high and migh-ty.

ETHEL: I could push her in the mud
                 But I'd get my clothes all mucky.
                 She'd go backwards with a thud
                 But then I'd feel all yucky

GEORGE: You don't want to be her friend
                 Cos you'd end up talking silly

BRIGGSY: And wearing lacy frocks!

GEORGE: You'd just end up feeling chilly

ETHEL: We'd ask you for dinner
                 But our portions are stingy

BRIGGSY: We won't have you round
                 You'd be nothing but whingy

BRIGGSY, GEORGE and ETHEL:
We live so free, a life without money
Don't mean we've got nothing, we have all we need
Fruit from the trees and eggs from the chickens
The world is our kitchen.
But you come along, like we're in the wrong
And you're all high and mighty.

ADA:
Please don't believe those things you say
I just would not dare to judge you that way
Because all I see when I look at you
Is the friendship I miss and want to share too
All I ask is we set judgement aside
Don't assume the worst

BRIGGSY: I'll chuck her in the dirt
                 Let's see her get all grubby

GEORGE: A grass stain on her skirt
                 Might stop her being snobby

ETHEL: She just wants to be our friend
                 She can't help talking proper
                 If she wants to play with us
                 What you gonna do to stop 'er?

(to Ada):   Do what George tells you
                 Or he'll give you a shiner
                 You may be the richest
                 But don't be a whiner

BRIGGSY, GEORGE and ETHEL:
We live so free, a life without money
Don't mean we've got nothing, we have all we need.
The view from the tree of fish in the river
The world is our playground.
But you come along, like we're in the wrong
And you're so high and mighty.
Push her, push her down in the mud.
Throw her, throw her down in the mud.
Push her down, push her down, push her down in the mud.

Throw her down, throw her down, throw her down
in the mud.

ADA: No please, don't… no please, don't…
Leave me alone, I meant no offence to you.
Just leave me be, and I will be done here soon.

BRIGGSY, GEORGE and ETHEL:
Chuck her in the mud, and we'll see the stuff she's made of!

*TOM NEWTON, aged 16, the blacksmith's apprentice and a sort of de facto
policeman among the village children, enters just as BRIGGSY shoves ADA,
making her fall backwards onto the ground. She breaks her fall with her
hands but hurts them. She drops her sketch-pad and starts to cry, her dreams
of making some new friends shattered. Tom, a gentle giant, is a big lad and
the only boy in the village Briggsy is afraid of.*

TOM: Hey! What's going on here?

*Briggsy, Ethel and George all freeze and stare at Tom. Ada, who is still there
on the ground, just looks up at Tom, unable to decide what to make of him.*

*BRIGGSY backs away from Ada and TOM marches up to him. Briggsy
bristles. Tom pushes him away.*

TOM: I said what's going on here, Briggs?

BRIGGSY: Nothing.

TOM: There'd better not be.

*Briggsy looks worried and runs off, followed hastily by Ethel and George.
Tom helps Ada to her feet. Fran picks up Ada's sketch-book and gives it to her.*

TOM: *(calling out after Briggs)* Not so big now, are you?

ADA: (to Tom) You're very strong.

TOM: I need to be. I work at the forge.

ADA: So are you the blacksmith?

TOM: *(good-humouredly)* No, I'm just his apprentice. My name's Tom Newton. I'm sixteen.

ADA: I'm Ada Byron. I'm fifteen. My mother Lady Byron's rented Bifrons House till Michaelmas, then we're going back to London. Thank you for rescuing me.

TOM: You're welcome. How are you?

ADA: Well, my hands hurt a bit. I'm all right, though. But I was already in trouble with my mama and now I've spoilt my dress as well.

TOM: It's just a bit of mud, it'll wash off. Why were you in trouble with your mother?

ADA: It was about my father.

TOM: Wait… Ada Byron? So your father's Lord Byron?

ADA: Yes. He died when I was only eight years old. I miss him so!

TOM: We studied one of his poems at school. I went to the village school until I was twelve. It was a brilliant poem, all about how the Assyrian army was destroyed by God. I even remember the first verse:

(singing)

'The Assyrian came down like the wolf on the fold, And his cohorts were gleaming in purple and gold; And the sheen of their spears was like stars on the sea, When the blue wave rolls nightly on deep Galilee.'

ADA: *(clapping her hands in excitement and then giving a pained look because they're still sore)*
That's my favourite of all of Papa's poems! It's wonderful you know it! …Papa died seven years ago, in Greece, of fever. I love him so and now I'll never see him! I never even met him. Mama was married to Papa for about a year but couldn't bear being with him any longer. So she left him

when I was just five weeks old. Mama still hates Papa even today. Oh, Mama doesn't like me wanting to fly.

TOM: Really? You want to fly?

ADA: Oh yes. I've a dream of building a steam-horse with wings.

TOM: A flying steam-engine?

ADA: Yes!

TOM: Ada, I don't want to be a wet blanket, but it wouldn't work.

ADA: Why not?

TOM: I'm interested in science. I try to read what I can about it. I know a little about steam-engines. I'm afraid they couldn't power a flying-machine.

ADA: But steam engines are really powerful!

TOM: Yes, but they're also really heavy, with the boiler and the pistons and everything. A steam-engine could never make enough power to lift itself off the ground.

ADA: Oh, I see.

TOM: I don't mean to disappoint you. I'm sure, one day, maybe even in our lifetimes, someone will invent an engine that's strong enough to use in a flying-machine.

ADA: So you think flying-machines could be invented and made to work?

TOM: Yes, with the right kind of engine.

ADA: It's wonderful you think flying's possible! Mama doesn't. She thinks I'm stupid for dreaming of flying.

TOM: No-one's stupid for dreaming, Ada. I dream of flying too. Sometimes I watch swallows and gulls soaring high above the village and I think, perhaps one day there'll be a machine people can fly in. I think of science so often. I don't want to be a blacksmith's apprentice all my life: I want to go to London one day and become an engineer and an inventor!

41

ADA: I want to be an inventor too! There's so much that's not been invented yet! Many new inventions will seem like magic until we know how they work! Oh, Tom, perhaps we could invent things together, and change the world!

SONG - THE WONDERS OF MACHINERY

ADA AND TOM

ADA: We could see our dreams come true,
The wonders of machinery,

TOM: We would totally enjoy the view
Of technological wizardry.

ADA: Metal birds with people aboard,

TOM:: Passengers at a thousand feet,

ADA: Skyharbours...

TOM: ... where the birds are stored.

ADA: Nose to tail, their flights complete.

TOM: A device beyond reason or rhyme,

ADA: A silvery incandescent sleigh,

TOM: Transporting us to another time -

ADA: We'd meet our childhood selves one day!

TOM: *(spoken)* How might that be possible, Ada?

ADA: *(spoken)* I'll explain later.

TOM: *(singing)* Hey, carriages without a horse
Travelling with enormous force -
Running on lamp-oil instead of oats...

ADA:	*(spoken)* Is anybody out there taking notes?
	(singing) Magic pictures on the wall,
	Beamed somehow to the village hall,
TOM:	Documentaries, contemporary dramas,
	Moving pictures sent to charm us,
ADA:	Let us pray they'll never harm us!
TOM:	*(spoken)* I'd protect you, Ada.
ADA:	*(spoken)* Oh, Tom…!
TOM:	*(singing)* A machine for talking to people who
	Live too far away to hear us shout.
ADA:	*(singing)* Talk to them the morning through…
ADA:	Or leave a message should they be out.
TOM:	*(spoken)* 'Leave a message should they be out?'
	But how, Ada?
ADA:	*(singing)* The wonders of machinery!
ADA AND TOM:	The wonders of machinery!
ADA AND TOM:	The wonders of machinery!
ADA AND TOM:	Oh, technological wizardry!
ADA:	We will see our dreams come true
	The wonders of machinery.
TOM:	We will totally enjoy the view
	Of technological wizardry,
ADA:	Metal birds with people aboard
TOM:	Passengers at a thousand feet,

ADA:	Skyharbours…
TOM:	… where the birds are stored.
ADA:	I'd wish to have a window seat!
TOM:	*(spoken)* Of course, madam!
ADA:	*(singing)* Oh, you are such a gentleman, Tom!

ADA AND TOM:	The wonders of machinery!
ADA AND TOM:	The wonders of machinery!
A DA AND TOM:	The wonders of machinery!
ADA AND TOM:	Oh, technological wizardry!

Ada and Tom finish the song feeling exhilarated, and briefly embrace then separate quickly in an embarrassed way, feeling they have gone too far. It is, after all, 1831.

Ada, suddenly afraid of her feelings for Tom, runs off.

TOM: *(shouting out after her)* I'll be here at seven o'clock this evening after work if you want to see me again!

But there is no reply, and Tom, full of despondency, exits.

SCENE 5 - THE DINING-ROOM AT BIFRONS HOUSE

About half an hour later. Ada and Lady Byron are having breakfast.

LADY BYRON: What on earth have you done to your dress? How did it get so dirty? And I can't believe you could be so late for breakfast.

ADA: I'm sorry, Mama. I've been busy.

LADY BYRON: Doing what?

ADA: I went out early this morning to sketch some birds so I could be sure of the shapes of their wings. I met three village children and I thought I could be friends with them. But they were horrible to me. They made fun of me and teased me and one of them threw me onto the ground. Then I was rescued.

LADY BYRON: By whom?

ADA: A boy called Tom. He's the village blacksmith's apprentice. He chased off the boy who threw me to the ground and was very nice to me.

LADY BYRON: 'Very nice' to you? What do you mean?

ADA: I mean he was friendly and we talked about inventing things together. Tom wants to go to London one day and become an engineer.

LADY BYRON: I will not have you associating with a black-smith's apprentice.

ADA: But Tom has great dreams of being an inventor, just as I do! He told me that a steam-engine is too heavy to provide power for a flying-machine, so it sounds as if unfortunately I'll have to abandon my idea of building a steam-horse.

LADY BYRON: Well, at least this urchin Tom has spoken good sense in one respect. Was this all that happened?

ADA: Tom isn't an urchin!

LADY BYRON: Whether or not he is really doesn't concern me. We've barely been in Kent for two weeks, and in that time you've been very rude to me in front of the Viscount of Whitstable and Lady Broadstairs, and by all accounts you've met a most unsuitable new acquaintance. It's clear to me that we coming down to Kent was a mistake. So I've decided to cancel my rental of this house. We're going back to London tomorrow.

ADA: We're going back to London? But I thought we were staying until Michaelmas! Michaelmas isn't until September!

LADY BYRON: I've changed my mind, Ada. And by the way, I've no intention of letting you meet this Tom again.

ADA: But I don't want to go back to London tomorrow! I want to spend the summer down here in Kent!

LADY BYRON: I know you do, but you're not going to. And by the way, you'll sleep in my bedroom tonight, so there's no danger of you slipping out to meet Tom.

ADA: It's not fair!

LADY BYRON: Welcome to life, Ada. Life isn't fair. If it was, I'd have had a husband I could rely on, instead of the one I got!

Ada gets up from the table, in tears.

LADY BYRON: Where are you going?

ADA: To my room. I'm going to play with Puff. She likes me, even if you don't!

Ada storms off.

SONG - HEARTS HURT AND ACHE

LADY BYRON

Ada sees me as cruel, I know,
Tougher than steel, colder than snow,
And yet - if she'd had the marriage I'd had -
I really don't believe she'd think me so bad.
At least I'm giving her a good education,
For women, knowledge is our salvation;
I know that Ada thinks I'm a witch,
But it's so hard to be a single mother, even if you're rich!

Hearts hurt and ache
But they never break;

All my love did he take,
Then threw it away
Like a mere bagatelle!
He left me in hell,
And that's where I dwell now, every single day.

I met a poet, a most wonderful man,
So wild and so flawed; I thought, 'I can
Reform him: I can make him see
That with fame, there comes responsibility.'
But oh, how I failed! He never understood;
He may have been great, but he was never good:
He was dangerous to know, he was mad, he was bad,
But Ada still adores him – it makes me so sad!

Hearts hurt and ache
But they never break;
All my love did he take,
Then threw it away
Like a mere bagatelle!
He left me in hell,
And that's where I dwell now, every single day.
Every single day.

A perpetual widow is what I am now;
It's a cold and bitter furrow he's left me to plough,
Spending my time in sorrow and alone,
Living in houses that are never a home.

Hearts hurt and ache
But they never break;
All my love did he take,
Then threw it away
Like a mere bagatelle!
He left me in hell,
And that's where I dwell now.

Hearts hurt and ache
But they never break;
All my love did he take,
Then threw it away
Like a mere bagatelle!
He left me in hell,
And that's where I dwell now.
Yes, that's where I dwell now,
Every single day.

At the end of the song, Lady Byron, in a violent pulse of emotion and with an anguished cry, dashes off.

SCENE 6 - A COUNTRY LANE NEAR BIFRONS

Tom runs on, dressed in his best, and takes out a watch from his pocket. It is obviously a prized possession; he handles it lovingly. A moment later, Ada runs on and joins him. She is desperately upset. She is carrying a small brown envelope.

TOM: Thank goodness you're here! My mother isn't too well; I had to make sure she was comfortable before I set out to meet you. I'm five minutes late. I thought you'd been and gone.

ADA: No, Tom, I'm here. I'm so sorry your mother's ill.

TOM: Thanks. I'm sure she'll feel better soon.

ADA: I'm glad to hear that. ...oh, Tom.

Ada bursts into tears.

TOM: What is it? What's the matter?

ADA: I can't see you any more! I can only stay with you a few minutes now. Mama will be furious if she knows I'm here at all.

TOM: Why?

48

ADA: She's forcing me to go back with her to London tomorrow.

TOM: But... I thought you and Lady Byron were going to be here in Kent until the autumn?

ADA: Oh, Tom, I did too! But Mama's angry with me. She says I'm disobedient, which I know I am, but only because she mostly tells me to do stupid things and doesn't take any interest in my scientific ambitions. Now listen, please listen. In this envelope there's a piece of paper. I've written my London address on it. You can write to me! But... I know posting letters to London is expensive, so I've put two sovereigns in the envelope.

TOM: I don't want your money, Ada!

ADA: You have to take it. I know you need to pay most of your wages to your mother, to support her and yourself. You're a good, hard-working boy and you look after your mother very well. Take the money, please. You won't be able to write to me otherwise, and I want you to. Please, please, take the envelope! I have to go back to London right away.

Tom unwillingly takes the envelope and puts it in one of his pockets.

ADA: Thank you, oh thank you! ... oh, will we ever meet again, do you think?

TOM: Yes, I'm sure of it! One day I'll come to London too and find work as an engineer, and then we'll get married.

ADA: Yes, yes, that would be wonderful! And you will write to me?

TOM: Darling Ada, yes of course. And I'll do extra jobs for people in the village, and earn more money, so that when the two sovereigns you kindly gave me have run out, I can still write to you.

ADA: Oh, Tom!

They embrace.

SONG - OH, TOM, MY LOVE!

ADA AND TOM

ADA: Oh, Tom, my love!
How ever can we part,
When deep romantic art
Brims in my heart?
Oh, Tom, my love!

TOM: Oh, Ada, dear!
How can I stay here
And know you're no longer near?
Your absence is what I fear,
Oh, Ada, dear!

ADA: Oh, Tom, my love!

TOM: Oh, Ada, dear!

ADA: How ever can we part,
When deep romantic art
Brims in my heart?

TOM: How am I to stay here
And know you're no longer near?
Your absence is what I fear.

Ada and Tom exchange a tentative kiss and the song now becomes more personal and more romantic.

ADA: Oh, leave me not to drown
In loneliness,
When I'm in London town
I'll think, my Kentish days were best!
And everywhere I go

In smart society
I'll miss you, darling, so,
I love you, dearest Tom,
I love you, dearest Tom - I'll wish you were in
London town with me.

TOM: Oh, Ada, please don't drown
In loneliness,
When you're in London town
I hope you'll think, your Kentish days were best!
And everywhere you go
In smart society
I'll miss you, darling, so,
I love you, Ada dear,
I love you, Ada dear - I'll wish I was in London town
with thee.

SONG - THE WONDERS OF
MACHINERY (REPRISE)

ADA AND TOM

ADA AND TOM *(singing together)*
We still hope to see our dreams come true,
The wonders of machinery,
We'd totally adore a view
Of technological scenery.

ADA
Carriages without a horse
Running on lamp-oil instead of oats,
Travelling with enormous force –
Is anybody taking notes?

ADA AND TOM

> Magic pictures on the wall,
> Documentaries, contemporary dramas,
> Beamed somehow to the village hall
> Which we could watch in our pyjamas.

ADA

> But none of this will matter much
> If you and I can't be together,
> I want to feel your lovely touch
> In sun, in rain, in every weather.

TOM

> No, none of this will matter much
> If you and I can't be together,
> I want to feel your lovely touch
> On grass, in woods, and in the heather.

ADA AND TOM

> Yes, technology's our second dream,
> For now we know we love each other
> Our love will be as hot as steam
> Despite my (TOM your) gorgon of a mother!
> Despite my (TOM your) gorgon of a mother!

They embrace.

SCENE 7 - THE DRAWING-ROOM OF LADY BYRON'S HOME AT ST JAMES'S SQUARE, LONDON

A year later. Wednesday, June 5 1833. Ada is now seventeen years old. She is reading. Lady Byron is doing embroidery.

(sung dialogue)

LADY BYRON: I hope you'll enjoy the Duke of Derbyshire's party this evening.

ADA: Do I really have to go?

LADY BYRON: Yes. I've accepted the invitation on behalf of both of us. Mr Babbage will be there. You might enjoy meeting him.

ADA: Mr who?

LADY BYRON: Babbage. Charles Babbage. One of the most distinguished mathematicians in London.
By all accounts he's completely mad, but I hear he can be entertaining.
The sort of fellow one wants to have at a soiree when it's raining.
He has for some years been working on a machine he calls the 'Difference Engine' or something like that.

ADA: You mean like a steam-engine?

LADY BYRON: Well, I gather that in the event his machine is completed
It will be powered by steam, yes.

ADA: What's it designed to do?

LADY BYRON: Carry out mathematical calculations
To make Britain arithmetical king of all the nations.

ADA: How very interesting.

LADY BYRON: I wouldn't get too excited about it if I were you.
I think we're about as likely to see a completed Difference Engine
As we are to see a dodo strutting about in St James's Park.

ADA: Well, I don't know about that, but the scientific men I've met at parties so far are a big disappointment.
All they care about is their next scientific appointment!
They all think women are too stupid to do much apart
From produce babies and comfort a man's heart.

LADY BYRON: Please don't speak with that vulgar spite!

ADA: Men just think women are there for ornamentation by day and fun at night!
Men don't want women to join their scientific fraternity!
They just want to dominate us for absolute eternity.

LADY BYRON: How many times have I told you not to speak in that crude fashion?
I think that fellow Tom filled you with a most unhealthy passion!

ADA: That's not true. It was love! It's been two years since I last saw him
And my hopeless heart can do nothing but adore him!

LADY BYRON: He should have had the sense not to court one of his betters,
And he never even replied to any of your letters!

ADA: Don't talk about Tom like that! Even though he didn't answer my letters, he was a lovely boy!

(spoken)

LADY BYRON: Please, Ada, I beg of you, don't humiliate me this evening by voicing these alarming opinions to the gentlemen we meet at the party!

ADA: Don't worry, Mama. I assure you I'll be the well-brought up, suppressed girl you want me to be.

LADY BYRON: *(unaware Ada is being ironic)* I'm relieved to hear it.

ADA: How old is Mr Babbage?

LADY BYRON: I'm not quite sure, I think about forty.

ADA: Does it ever occur to you that I might one day want to go to a party that is attended by at least one young gentlemen of my own age?

LADY BYRON: I'll arrange for you to meet such a person when I judge the time is right. In the meantime, I wish you to become better known in elegant London society.

ADA: I still miss Tom so much.

LADY BYRON: Yes, well, he was a typical man, wasn't he? He promised to be loyal to you, but he wasn't. He didn't write you a single letter, did he?

ADA: No. He gave me his address, and I wrote twenty-six letters to him, but he never replied to any of them.

LADY BYRON: That's only because you don't understand men. If you knew the male sex as I do, you'd expect to be disappointed by them.

SONG - WHEN A MAN SAYS HE LOVES YOU, DON'T BELIEVE HIM!

LADY BYRON

When a man says he loves you, don't believe him!
He'll woo you and promise you a glorious life
Full of high purpose, and things to believe in
But woe betide you if you decide to be… his wife,
Woe betide you if you decide to be his wife!
When a man says you're lovely, it's a code
To open a gate leading to a dangerous road
And down to the most sinister of fields
Where he'll grab at your frock, and so he his purpose reveals!
And nine months later you'll be holding his baby,
Will he ever visit you? No, not even maybe.
Men are selfish, and their appetite is king,
That's absolutely true, whether you speak or choose to sing.
And if you try to win his heart by cooking
He'll kiss the kitchen-maid when you're not looking!
Men aren't even as necessary as thought,
Their reproductive material could easily be bought!
Ada, one day please write a thesis
On the benefits to women of parthenogenesis!

(spoken)

ADA: Parthenogenesis, Mama? What's that?

LADY BYRON: I presume it's defined in Dr Johnson's *Dictionary*, that is, if he was man enough to include it!

ADA: Mama, there must surely be some trustworthy men in the world.

LADY BYRON: I doubt it. Now, we should start to dress for the party. I've asked Walker to have the carriage ready by eight o'clock.

ADA: *Can't* I stay at home and read?

LADY BYRON: No, you're coming with me. I've no intention of going to the party by myself. I did quite enough of that when I was married to your father!

SCENE 8 - A ROOM IN THE DUKE OF DERBYSHIRE'S HOUSE IN KENSINGTON, LONDON

As Lady Byron and Ada come into the room, CHARLES BABBAGE, aged forty-one, is in a sotto voce conversation with the Viscount of Whitstable, who is trying his best to understand him. There are a few OTHER GUESTS, including the DUKE OF DERBYSHIRE, in the room.

BABBAGE: *(to the Viscount)* As for painting the outside of a house, that involves calculating by the index minus one. Of course, I am assuming revenue to be a function.

THE VISCOUNT OF WHISTABLE: I'm not quite sure what you mean, Babbage.

The Viscount of Whitstable sees Lady Byron and Ada.

VISCOUNT OF WHITSTABLE: *(to Babbage)* Would you please excuse me for a moment?

BABBAGE: Of course.

Babbage starts talking sotto voce to the Duke of Derbyshire.

VISCOUNT OF WHITSTABLE: *(to Lady Byron and Ada)* My dear Lady Byron and Ada! How delightful it is to see you both again!

LADY BYRON: Thank you, Viscount. The feeling is certainly mutual.

VISCOUNT OF WHITSTABLE: *(to Lady Byron)* It's been much too long. You both look very well. *(to Ada)* What about your flying steam-horse, my dear? Did it ever get off the ground?

ADA: Alas, no. Mama was very much opposed to my experiments in flight.

LADY BYRON: Yes, Ada, and that's why you've survived beyond your seventeenth birthday.

VISCOUNT OF WHITSTABLE: *(to Ada)* I imagine you find scientific men a great inspiration?

ADA: I wish I could say I did, sir, but not wishing to be rude, I'm afraid I don't. Indeed, if the scientific men I've met so far are representative of the best London can offer, I'm afraid to say it's scarcely surprising that the most ingenious machine in the world isn't British but French!

VISCOUNT OF WHITSTABLE: The French have an advantage over us in machinery? I hope not.

ADA: But they do, sir.

VISCOUNT OF WHITSTABLE: Which French machine do you mean?

ADA: The Jacquard loom, sir. It permits images as beautiful as oil paintings to be woven by a weaver working alone.

SONG - THE JACQUARD LOOM

ADA

(at first Ada sings in a measured scientific way)

Jacquard's machine is a very strange thing,
What does it do, does it fly, or cook or sing?
Just what's the secret of its mysterious art?
In what branch of science does it play a magic part?

In fact I think you'll all be relieved
To hear it does nothing more dangerous than weave.
Its inventor, Monsieur Jacquard, was a weaver in France
Who felt the old draw-loom a ridiculous prance
And decided it was time to put a total stop
To a weaver sitting at the loom and one more on the top,
And thought of the answer again and again -
Replace the draw-boy with a punched-card chain!

(now Ada sings in a more expansive, lyrical tone)

And it weaves beautiful pictures and all of them seem
To be not of this world but on the edge of a dream.
They resemble oil paintings by a brilliant old master -
And the Jacquard loom weaves them faster and faster!
Beautiful paintings for kings, queens and earls,
More precious than sapphires, diamonds and pearls.

(the instructional tone again)

But a question changed the way the machine looked in my eyes
Is the Jacquard loom a computer in disguise?
By 'computer' I don't mean clerks toiling all day
At mental arithmetic for miserable pay,
I mean something else, a machine that can think
That notion's a well of thought from which I drink.

(the lyrical tone)

And it weaves beautiful pictures and all of them seem
To be not of this world but on the edge of a dream,
They resemble oil paintings by a brilliant old master -
And the Jacquard loom weaves them faster and faster!
Beautiful paintings for kings, queens and earls,
More precious than sapphires, diamonds and pearls.
Beautiful pictures for kings, queens and earls,
More precious than sapphires, diamonds and pearls!

BABBAGE applauds this song with particular enthusiasm.

VISCOUNT OF WHITSTABLE: Lady Byron, may I introduce Charles Babbage to you? He is a friend of mine, and the inventor of the famous Difference Engine, a remarkable calculating-machine, made from cogwheels.

LADY BYRON: Good evening, Mr Babbage.

THE VISCOUNT OF WHITSTABLE: And this is Lady Byron's daughter, Ada.

BABBAGE: *(to Lady Byron)* I'm pleased to meet you both. I know, of course, something of your life story, Lady Byron, and I have much sympathy for you.

(to Ada) Miss Byron, it's most interesting that you find the Jacquard loom so remarkable. I'm familiar with Monsieur Jacquard's invention myself, but you are the first lady I've ever met who is.

THE VISCOUNT OF WHITSTABLE: Come, dear Lady Byron, let me introduce you to our host, the Duke of Derbyshire. I fear Babbage's and Ada's conversation will soon become too scientific for me to understand it!

The viscount steers Lady Byron over to the Duke of Derbyshire, leaving Ada and Babbage tête-à-tête in the foreground.

ADA: Thank you for your kind words, Mr Babbage.

BABBAGE: So are you now out in society?

ADA: Yes. I'm seventeen years old and was recently presented at court to King William and Queen Adelaide.

BABBAGE: It's a pleasure for me to talk to you, Miss Byron. I have hardly any experience of speaking with young ladies except to my daughter Georgie.

ADA: Oh, you have a daughter. How old is she?

BABBAGE: Fifteen on July the seventeenth.

ADA: Is she interested in mathematics?

BABBAGE: No, Miss Byron, Georgie is not merely *interested* in it but is crazed with the subject.

ADA: I'd love to meet her!

BABBAGE: I hope you shall.

ADA: Why do you call it a Difference Engine?

BABBAGE: Well, in the science of mathematics there is something known as a mathematical series, which is...

ADA: (*interrupting*) A set of terms in ordered succession. I'm passionate about mathematics too, Mr Babbage.

BABBAGE: Oh, I see, you understand! Excellent! Well, the Difference Engine uses the Method of Differences to simplify the process of calculating a long series of mathematical terms.

ADA: Oh I see! And of course if a machine is carrying out the large quantity of additions, these will never be irksome to the clerks because the machine is doing the work.

BABBAGE: Yes! But, Miss Byron when you told us about the Jacquard loom you spoke of a 'computer': a machine that could calculate, not a clerk at all!

ADA: Exactly!

SONG - WHAT AN AMAZING IDEA –
A COMPUTER!

ADA AND BABBAGE

BABBAGE
What an amazing idea, a computer!
A machine that's mechanically cuter
Than any device I intended.
I didn't know what I'd invented!

ADA
Sometimes we don't know what we're doing,
We don't know what magic we're brewing.
We think we're being evolutionary,
When in fact we're being revolutionary.

BABBAGE
What an amazing idea, a computer!
A machine that would surely suit a
Time that might still be unborn,
Yet maybe we're now at its dawn?

I thought a 'computer' could only be a clerk,
But thanks to you, I see I was totally in the dark.
When you spoke of Monsieur Jacquard's creation,
I thought you were demeaning our nation.

ADA
No, I was just saying that there's surely room
For a loom that isn't only a loom,
And instead of weaving landscapes and flowers
It could have mathematical powers!

ADA
What an amazing idea, a computer!
Not a clerk, but mechanically neuter;
It doesn't need meals or water
And it would never run off with your daughter!

BABBAGE AND ADA TOGETHER
What an amazing idea, a computer!
It might usher in a new future
Where mankind masters information –
That would call for a great celebration!

ADA: So... the Difference Engine would make the calculations with mechanical precision, removing all possibility of human error?

BABBAGE: Exactly. I am so impressed someone so young can understand my work so well!

ADA: I'm only seventeen, it's true. But I believe that when people share a passionate interest in some fascinating subject such as maths, differences of age are irrelevant.

BABBAGE: I'm sure you're right. The work I'm doing is vitally important. Mathematical tables are our only way of making complex calculations such as those needed in navigation, in construction, in all the practical branches of science. Yet the tables are produced manually by human clerks rather than the mechanical ones you propose and it is impossible for the clerks to avoid human errors.

ADA: What would the consequences of those errors be?

BABBAGE: Oh, Miss Byron, they are like sunken rocks at sea!

SONG - SUNKEN ROCKS AT SEA

BABBAGE

Those sunken rocks at sea
Are not rocks literally:
They lurk in a mathematical table,
Lead us up the garden path
In applied and pure maths,
Make everything unstable.

We can have no confidence in calculation –
Such a disaster for a scientific nation!

Those sunken rocks at sea
Obsess and torture me –
That's why I'm seen as crazy by my neighbours!
But I just want to bring us light
And the certainty we're right –
That's the whole aim of my labours.

I believe I have an excellent chance of success –
Failure doesn't live at my address.
No, failure doesn't live at my address!

But oh, my work incurs such high costs!
Right now there's no profit, only loss.
I inherited a hundred thousand pounds,
But my cogwheels have rather ground it down.

And my children must be provided for –
I can hardly do that if I'm poor!
No, I can hardly do that if I'm poor!

I don't want it to turn out to be
That those sunken rocks have sunk me!

No, I don't want it to turn out to be
That those sunken rocks have sunk me!

No, I don't want it to turn out to be
That those sunken rocks have sunk me!

No, I don't want it to turn out to be
That those sunken rocks have sunk me!

ADA: I love your passion for your work! Your wife must be a happy woman to have a husband with such an important ambition, and who is so ardent about it!

BABBAGE: There's no longer a Mrs Babbage, I'm afraid. My wife Georgiana died almost six years ago. My beloved Georgie - my only daughter - was named after her. Yes, Georgie is my greatest comfort now.

ADA: You have no other comforts?

BABBAGE: Only my work, Miss Byron.

ADA: I should love to see your Difference Engine, and to meet Georgie.

BABBAGE: Then come to my house at noon tomorrow at Dorset Street, off Manchester Square, and you can meet both of them.

SCENE 9 - THE DRAWING-ROOM OF BABBAGE'S HOUSE IN DORSET STREET. THE FOLLOWING DAY

This is a room inhabited by the eccentric mathematician Babbage; there are papers and books scattered on the floor; the furniture is quality but scruffy, the room looks as though it hasn't been tidied for several years.

Babbage and Ada, already friends, enter the room together in calm and thoughtful conversation, Babbage leading the way.

BABBAGE: We'll take tea and cake in here. I'm sorry; I know the room is untidy but I assure you, I know where everything is. So, what did you think of the Difference Engine?

ADA: Oh, Mr Babbage!

BABBAGE: I'm so sorry if it bored you. I need to remember that just because my work enthrals me, that doesn't mean that anybody else will necessarily find it of interest.

ADA: Bored? You really think I find it boring! Oh, Mr Babbage, the machine is wonderful! It's like a thinking-machine! A machine of the mind!

BABBAGE: Really, you are too kind! But please remember that the Difference Engine hasn't yet been completed. What you saw is only one-seventh of it, but even that section can carry out numerous calculations.

ADA: Yes, I understand that. But what's preventing you from finishing it?

BABBAGE: Mainly the problem of making enough completely accurate identical cogwheels that are completely accurate. There's something else, too. I'm planning another machine, one whose aims completely supersede the Difference Engine and which will render it obsolete.

ADA: What machine's that?

But before Babbage can reply, his daughter GEORGIE, fourteen years old, vivacious, pretty, skips gaily into the room and answers Babbage's question.

GEORGIE: It's called the Analytical Engine. It's even more extraordinary than the Difference Engine! The Difference Engine was only designed to calculate numbers for mathematical tables, but the Analytical Engine could calculate absolutely everything!

BABBAGE: My beloved daughter is good enough to speak well of the new machine I'm working on.

GEORGIE: Papa, anyone who truly knows about the Analytical Engine will speak highly of it!

ADA: Georgie, I'm Ada Byron. I'm delighted to meet you.

Ada goes up to Georgie and they shake hands.

GEORGIE: I've heard of your own papa, of course. I so love his poetry. Are you as passionate and imaginative as he was?

ADA: I try to be all those things, but my mama usually does her best to stop me.

BABBAGE: My dear young ladies, please excuse me now. I need to write some letters. Will you be all right by yourselves?

GEORGIE: Oh, yes, Papa. Miss Byron and I shall speak of mathematics… and other things.

BABBAGE: Very well, but please, my dear, don't involve our distinguished guest in any unseemly conversation.

GEORGIE: As if I would, Papa!

Babbage smiles, and leaves the room.

GEORGIE: Do tell me, Miss Byron, do you like mathematics?

ADA: I love it. But please, Georgie, you must call me Ada. I'm a little older than you, I know, but 'Miss Byron' sounds so terribly formal.

GEORGIE: Yes of course. Thank you, Ada. I myself was named for my poor mama, Georgiana, who died I was only eight years old. Dear Ada, how old are you?

ADA: Seventeen. Like you, I lost a parent when I was only eight. As you know, that was my papa, Lord Byron.

GEORGIE: Yes, we have so much in common. I'm fourteen, by the way. Shall we be best friends?

ADA: I'd love that. I've never had a friend of my own age.

GEORGIE: Or even approximately so! …Do you know what *omnia vincit amor* means?

ADA: Yes. 'Love conquers all.'

GEORGIE: Do you think it does?

ADA: Yes, I think so. Without love, nothing is worthwhile.

GEORGIE: Is there a beau in your life?

ADA: Not now, though there once was.

GEORGIE: Who was he? A young lord or prince?

ADA: My dear Georgie, he was neither. He was a village boy I used to know, when I was staying at a house near Canterbury in Kent.

GEORGIE: Please tell me about him.

SONG - A DREAM OF TOM

[This song is inspired by Princess Mi's solo in Franz Lehar's *The Land of Smiles*.]

ADA AND GEORGIE

ADA
It's always Tom of whom I'm thinking
And no, G, I've not been drinking!
Tom's the one I love,
Ordained from above.

In the village he was thoughtful
Saved me from some kids quite awful
Who pushed me on the grass
Where I hurt my… hands.

So I dream, of Tom, all day, he fills my soul completely
His voice, of course, it still sounds oh so sweetly,
He's all I want in a man
He's absolutely part of who I am.

How I miss him how I love him how I dream of him continually! He's my destiny, I have to say,

He's my dream, my girlish madness, when I miss him I'm full of sadness, and

I miss him every single day!

He's the one who'd chase my blues away...

He's the one I pray to when I pray...

How I miss him how I love him how I dream of him continually! He's my destiny, I have to say,

I wish he could come and see me hold me kiss me love me completely but Mama would only chase him away!

GEORGIE

If he's strong and fit she'd likely bray,

'Come and dance with me, Tom, oh, let's sway!'

ADA

But she might consume him like her prey!

Meanwhile this is what *I* want to say...

'Tom my darling, you're so charming, come here now and don't be barmy, yes, it's June but let's pretend it's May!'

GEORGIE *(singing)*

I wouldn't believe this if it were in a play!

ADA *(singing)*

What can I do to make this pain go away?

GEORGIE

Write to him you hopeless sweetie tell him you want him completely and you need him to drive your pain away!

ADA

If I did that I wonder what he'd say...

(spoken)

But anyway…

(singing)

How I miss him how I love him how I dream of him continually! He's my destiny, I have to say,

He's my dream, my girlish madness, when I miss him I'm full of sadness, and

I miss him every single day!

He's the one who'd chase my blues away!

He's the one I pray to when I pray!

Yes, he's the one I pray to when I pray!

(spoken)

ADA: But you see, dear Georgi. I did write to Tom, many times, after I got back to London and he was still in Kent. But he never, ever, answered my letters.

GEORGIE: Oh, Ada, I'm so sorry to hear that! Men can sometimes be so ungrateful for the love we give them!

ADA: But you're so young, how would you know about that?

GEORGIE: I don't. But I've read about it in so many novels…

She puts her arm around Ada and they sadly exit.

SCENE 10 - THE DRAWING-ROOM OF LADY BYRON'S HOME AT ST JAMES'S SQUARE, LONDON

A few weeks later. Ada is reading. Lady Byron is doing embroidery.

LADY BYRON: Ada, it is time to find you a husband. Marriage will quieten you down. You will have to love, honour and obey your husband… and especially the latter.

ADA: Well, all right, as long as my husband will love honour and obey me too! I was wondering whether Mr Babbage might be interested in marrying me. He is after all, a widower, and I am sure he gets lonely. And I very much like his daughter Georgie. She has become a great friend of mine.

LADY BYRON: Babbage has a daughter? The poor girl! Does she have a face like a cogwheel?

ADA: No, Georgie is extremely pretty…

LADY BYRON: Well, whatever she may be like, of course you're not going to marry Babbage. He is twenty-four years older than you, and moreover it is by now quite clear to me that he is completely mad and utterly unsuitable as a husband for you. Babbage is the only man I've ever met who makes your late father seem relatively normal. No, I shall arrange for you to be introduced to some suitable young men.

ADA: Very well, Mama… as Tom, the man I love, never replied to any of my letters, and as I suppose I shall never see him again, I don't much mind whom I marry, really. Mama, do your worst! Please, bring them on!

The lights dim and LORD WORTHING enters. He is a brainless beau with ornate clothes and a foppish look about him.

LORD WORTHING: *(in a silly posh accent)* Oh, hello, *(though it sounds more like 'air hair lair')* my dear Miss Byron!
Lady Byron, still visible at one side of, views proceedings.

ADA: Hello, Lord Worthing.

Lord Worthing goes up to Ada and looks at her from various angles.

LORD WORTHING: Heavens! You really are a fine filly. Dashed glad to meet you.

ADA: I'm pleased to meet you too, Lord Worthing.

Lord Worthing doesn't seem to know what to say. He looks awkward. Then he thinks of something.

LORD WORTHING: I say, Miss Byron, do you like quadrilles?

ADA: Not really. I'm not very interested in dancing. I find it rather dull.

LORD WORTHING: You don't like dancing? Are you serious?

ADA: I'm afraid so.

LORD WORTHING: What about hunting?

ADA: Hunting? You mean foxes?

(sung dialogue)

WORTHING: Yes! Foxes, otters, hares. The thrill of the chase!

ADA: I prefer quadratic equations, algebra to a ten base!

WORTHING: What about shooting! A crisp dawn, the beaters at work!

ADA: I prefer mathematical puzzles I never would shirk.

WORTHING: The grouse rising high from the heather.

ADA: I'll solve geometrical puzzles in all kinds of weather.

WORTHING:
A fine old rare port. Hunting foxes with hounds.
Roast pheasant! Game pie! A walk round our grounds.
A ride in my open coach in the crisp spring air.
Going to banquets and saying 'air, hair, lair!'
Inspecting the pheasant-traps to see what they've caught:
A peasant or two, going where they shouldn't ought!

ADA:
Shooting defenceless creatures is neither noble nor new,
It would be much better sport if the birds were armed too!
Roast pheasant and partridge, I'd rule them right out
All they'd do is bring me on an attack of gout.

LORD WORTHING: Perhaps you'll come to see me next week? I'll get a grouse in the oven.

ADA: Sorry, I'm staying in, and Mama will be at her coven.

Lord Worthing exits sorrowfully.

WILLIAM, LORD KING enters. Smartly-dressed and standing to attention, he answers questions put to him by Lady Byron.

LADY BYRON: Name?

WILLIAM: William, Lord King.

LADY BYRON: Is your title more than a hundred years old?

WILLIAM: I'm glad to say it is, Lady Byron.

LADY BYRON: Very good. Your age?

WILLIAM: Thirty.

LADY BYRON: Occupation?

WILLIAM: Unemployed but wealthy aristocrat.

LADY BYRON: Excellent. Your wealth?

WILLIAM: Very substantial.

LADY BYRON: Your prospects?

WILLIAM: I confidently expect to become the Earl of Lovelace in three years' time.

LADY BYRON: Intellectual achievements?

WILLIAM: I can play polo.

LADY BYRON: Even better!

William exits.

LADY BYRON: Ada!

ADA: Yes, Mama?

LADY BYRON: You are to marry William, Lord King.

ADA: William?

LADY BYRON: Yes.

ADA: Mama, he is a nice enough man, but… listen, I don't love William. I still love Tom.

LADY BYRON: Don't be absurd. That country bumpkin! He didn't answer a single one of your letters, did he?

ADA: No, but…

LADY BYRON: You're being absurd, just like your father! Ada, I'm not supporting you financially any more, and that's that. Lord King is a good man. I'm not saying he is a man with a first-class mind, but he will look after you and I know he loves you. He is also extremely rich, not an impoverished blacksmith's apprentice like Tom was! The sooner you forget about Tom completely, the better! I'm sure you'll never see him again! Forget Tom, do you understand!

Lady Byron strides off in a temper.

Ada, feeling hopeless, gives a sigh.

SONG - OH FUTURE DWELLERS, WHEN YOU THINK OF ME

ADA

Oh future dwellers, when you think of me,
Don't blame me for my endless struggle,
I want so much to be who I can be
And my responsibilities all juggle.
I yearn to forge an intellectual career
And live a life of ingenious invention
Give comfort to the people to me dear
Yes, science and true love, they were my intention.

But saying 'forge' just makes me think of Tom,
And did he simply ignore my letters?
I wonder what exactly I've done wrong,
Or did he think Love really should forget us?
I may as well marry William, I suppose;
He is a good man and he cares about me,
Tom's love for me is obviously at a close
And I don't want Mama any more to tout me.
I think I'll never achieve a mental life
That's been my dream, never totally forsaken
But now I need to become a noble's wife
And yet my dream seems just as strong, if very shaken.
But shall I have to greet my grave unknown,
Yet another loser who never made it,
Is there some meaning here we haven't shown,
Will my life mean nothing after I've played it?
Will all my hopes and dreams turn dark and lost,
Will all the love I had fade into dust
Will there ever be any profit, only cost,
Will my machines get jammed and start to rust?
No, surely not, for I believe I may
Be known beyond my death, one wondrous day,
I believe I'll invent something worthwhile
And with poetical science walk down a mystic aisle!

Ada weeps again briefly then exit.

SCENE 11 - A LAKESIDE IN THE GROUNDS OF OCKHAM, A STATELY HOME IN SURREY OWNED BY WILLIAM

Two months later. A summer day. William and Ada are sitting in cane chairs next to each other. There is a picnic on a little table next to them.

WILLIAM: How wonderful it is here by the lake!

ADA: It's lovely. I can't believe how big the grounds of your house are here in Surrey.

WILLIAM: Yes, I do like being rich even if I didn't actually do anything to earn the money, and I love having a gorgeous stately home to live in and lots of servants.

(beat)

I realise we've only known each other for only about a month, but… I've grown truly fond of you, Miss Byron.

ADA: William, I've told you. Call me Ada.

WILLIAM: Thank you… Ada. As… as I say. I've grown very fond of you and… and…

He falls silent with nervousness.

ADA: William, relax. Try the lobster salad. It's delicious. What a lovely view we have!

WILLIAM: Yes, but nothing is as lovely as you.

He gets off his chair, and goes down on his hands and knees to Ada.

I do love you, Miss Byron… I mean Ada.

ADA: I know you do.

WILLIAM: But I worry about you. You're so full of energy for wanting to invent things, I really applaud that. You're so passionate about wanting to have a life of the mind. I applaud that too.

ADA: Why?

WILLIAM: Because I love you.

(Sung dialogue)

I know I'm no great intellectual,

I got most of my learning by rote,
I'm only moderately effectual,
But on you, dearest, I truly dote.
And that's why I'm telling you, Ada –
My darling, beloved wife to be,
This world isn't one where women have played a
Part in furthering scientific history.

ADA: I know, William, but that's the whole point!
Men simply haven't given us the chance!
They think we're only good for ordering a beef joint
And looking pretty and partnering them in a dance.
There's so much I want to do for science,
So many machines that are not yet invented,
In me maths and poetry create an alliance,
When I've achieved something great I'll be contented.

WILLIAM: But why break your heart in that ambition
When you could live a life of family bliss?
Look at Babbage, he's still basically a failure
Despite years of effort and struggle.
Why be like him? Why not let yourself be happy?

ADA: I want to be happy just as you want me to be,
But I can't unless I'm going to be me!
And that means an Ada with a hope of making a mark
On the practical sciences before I enter the dark.

WILLIAM: I respect your feelings,
But many men think women have no place at all
In the practical science heroism roll call.

ADA: But they're wrong, we women have so much to give
To the world of invention, and perhaps, being women
We'll have insights that in men aren't even beginning!

WILLIAM: But Ada, please don't break your heart.

ADA: You have to believe in me or else we must part.

WILLIAM: No! I love you and I'll always be by your side,
I want you to be happy, your sadness I can't abide.

ADA: Then be my helpmate in my quest to be
A woman who brings to science the romance of poetry!

WILLIAM: I shall. Darling I shall. Then will you be my wife?

ADA: Oh, William, yes of course, if it will make you happy!

SCENE 12 - ADA AND WILLIAM'S WEDDING INSIDE A CHURCH

Wedding music.

A VICAR, the REVEREND CUSWORTH, is officiating at the wedding of Ada and William. Lady Byron, Babbage and Georgie are among various WEDDING GUESTS. The guests also include a MYSTERIOUS MALE GUEST, who stands to one side, and whose face we can't see as his large top hat and his high shirt collars, obscure it. Ada doesn't notice him.

REVEREND CUSWORTH: Do you, William, Lord King, take Ada Byron to be your lawful wedded wife?

WILLIAM: I certainly do.

REVEREND CUSWORTH: Do you, Ada Byron, take William, Lord King, to be your lawful wedded husband?

ADA: *(after a moment's hesitation)* Yes, I do.

REVEREND CUSWORTH: (to William) You may kiss the bride.

William kisses Ada.

SONG - HE'S NOT THE ONE SHE REALLY WANTS!

Ada, William, Lady Byron and the vicar stay in the background while various guests sing in a gossipy was as if passing secrets to each other.

MALE GUEST ONE
He's not the one she really wants, but it certainly can't be bad
To think that all her kids will have an aristo for a dad!

LADY GUEST ONE (to LADY GUEST TWO)
I'd never have hesitated if I'd been asked to say 'I do',
He's handsome, rich and manly, I bet you wish he were marrying you!

LADY GUEST TWO
You've won your bet, my dear, I wouldn't see it as a disgrace
To think that in a year or two I'd be Lady Lovelace!

MALE GUEST TWO
I don't suppose she needs the cash, her mother's immensely rich.
And it's not as if dear Ada was born in poverty in a ditch.
But I've heard she's got strange ideas way beyond her station
Of doing her best to advance the science in our scientific nation.

MALE GUEST ONE
Don't worry, she'll be tamed by the needs of married life
And I think there's every chance she'll be an obedient wife,

ALL GUESTS
He's not the one she really wants!
He's not the one she really wants!

He's not the one she really wants!
He's not the one she really wants!
No no no!
He's not the one she really wants!
Not the one she really wants!
He's not the one she really wants!

Married, Ada and William slowly leave, accompanied by everyone but the Mysterious Guest, to a musical accompaniment.

The Mysterious Guest is now alone. He pulls his shirt collars down and takes his top hat off. We see that it is Tom.

TOM: Oh, Ada, now I've lost you for ever!

CURTAIN

ACT 2

SCENE 1 - A LONDON STREET

A few weeks later.

> *The CHORUS composed of FOUR MEN and*
> *FOUR WOMEN dressed in nineteenth-century*
> *outfits comes on again.*

SONG - SO MAYBE YOU THINK ADA'S MARRIAGE WILL TAME HER?

[to the same tune as 'The Glorious Industrial Revolution']

CHORUS OF MEN AND WOMEN
So maybe you think Ada's marriage will tame her?
But even if you don't, I doubt you'll really blame her
For using her beauty and charm to find a husband
Especially after Lady Byron has totally bludgeoned
Poor Ada into saying 'yes' at the altar -
And so it seems William has her by the halter -
But, knowing Ada now, as I surely think you do,
She'll have a lot of fun even if to hubby she stays true!

WOMAN CHORUS MEMBER 1
We like our husbands to love us and arouse us,
As long as they remember it's the wife who wears the trousers!

MAN CHORUS MEMBER 1
Don't spare the rod, it'll spoil the wife,
And then we'd have the most horribly hen-pecked life!

WOMAN CHORUS MEMBER 2
'Hen-pecked'? Think yourselves lucky we talk to you at all,
When your conversational powers - *and* other things - are rather small!

CHORUS OF MEN

All women need a manly husband who will guide them,
And who's taught and instructed them from the moment he first eyed them.
Yes - we grant our wives freedom to pick and to choose...
Ingredients which the cook will subsequently use.
A man's a master of the home, the Englishman's proud castle,
A wife's a minor personage, a sort of beloved vassal.
In truth, marriage really only benefits the lady
Though it might make us less devoted to assignations that are shady.
After all, who needs to go to seek illicit pleasures
When in the marital bedroom there need be no half-measures!

CHORUS OF WOMEN

Oh, of course you proclaim your insatiable lasciviousness -
If only you were truly able thoroughly to pleasure us!
It's a great shame that so often, after you reach your conclusion
We're left to reflect that happy marriage may be an illusion!
But no doubt, at your club, over a double whisky and water,
You say your wife adores you and you totally taught her
Just what being a women really means, and now she's in your thrall,
When the truth often is, you can hardly perform at all!
But no, we keep quiet, about marital frustration –
After all, aren't we doing a womanly service for the nation?
'Lie back and think of England,' that's what Mummy often said,
And too often it's a synopsis of life in a marital bed!

The chorus of men and women exit

SCENE 2 - BABBAGE'S DRAWING-ROOM AT HIS HOME ON DORSET STREET, LONDON

A few weeks later. Ada and Georgie are sitting at a table, studying a large globe. There is a comfortable-looking sofa in the room and several chairs.

GEORGIE: *(pointing to the United States)* I'd love to go to the United States someday, see the bison and live in a wigwam!

(turning the globe so she can touch China)

Or perhaps China would be even more fun. We could walk along the Great Wall, and eat Thousand Year Old Eggs, though they don't sound very nice to me. I think three minutes in the saucepan is quite long enough for any egg. ...Oh, Ada, it was a wonderful wedding. Papa and I so enjoyed it. ...Well, I enjoyed it anyway. Papa was a little... never mind. What does it feel like to be married?

ADA: Rather like it was before I was married, but now I sleep in a bigger bed.

GEORGIE: I do wish you'd married Papa and not William. Papa is a trifle pedantic, I know, but he can be good fun. You could have worked on his machines together.

ADA: I know. Georgie, I did think of it, in fact, but unfortunately Mama wouldn't hear of it. Besides, do you really think Mr Babbage would have wanted to marry me?

GEORGIE: I don't know. Very possibly yes. Papa's never spoken to me of his feelings. I think he still loves Mama, but I'm sure he is very fond of you too.

ADA: But he's never told me he is.

GEORGIE: He never would! Deep down he's terribly shy. Besides, he knows your mother would never have agreed.

ADA: That's right. She wouldn't.

GEORGIE: It's too hot to study the globe. Why don't we walk to the Serpentine and take a rowing-boat?

ADA: What a lovely idea!

GEORGIE: But please let me row!

ADA: Of course you can.

Babbage enters the room in his usual energetic and flustered state.

BABBAGE: Georgie, I want to plan a set of navigational calculations. I was wondering if you know where my globe might be?

He sees it.

BABBAGE: Oh, there it is.

GEORGIE: Papa, I'm thinking of travelling to distant lands.

BABBAGE: Oh please don't do that. I would be exceedingly lonely without you, my darling girl.

GEORGIE: Ada would come with me.

BABBAGE: Then I would be lonelier still. *(Seeing Ada)* I didn't know you were here... Lady King.

ADA: I didn't want to disturb you in your work, so I came in through the servant's entrance. Georgie told me you're particularly busy at present. Charles, you can still call me 'Ada', you know. I may be married, but we are still good friends.

BABBAGE: Very well... Ada. I trust you are enjoying married life?

ADA: Oh, yes, it's pleasant not to be obliged to live with my mother any more, and to have a husband who does everything I say.

(in a consciously bright tone)

Georgie and I are going to take a boat on the Serpentine. Why not join us?

BABBAGE: I thank you... but I need to work.

GEORGIE: Oh, Papa! You are always working!

BABBAGE: I know, but my Engines take up most of my time, and especially, at the moment, my Difference Engine makes the most pressing demands upon me.

ADA: Georgie and I would love to spend more time with you. Oh, well… come on, Georgie! We'll see you later, Charles.

GEORGIE: Goodbye, Papa!

Ada and Georgie leave jauntily on their way to the Serpentine.

Babbage watches them go.

SONG - MAY I NEVER FALL PREY TO IRRATIONAL EMOTION

BABBAGE

Oh may I never fall prey to irrational emotion
That stirs my wretched heart like a typhoon stirs the ocean
And wastes my precious time with ridiculous commotion
Making me a slave to love's treacherous sweet potion.

The world so badly needs my cogwheel calculation
Those sunken rocks I mentioned plague almost every nation,
Devotion to my goal is my glorious earthly station
Understanding errors and destroying their causation.

Ada my wife, what a joy that would've been!
I the cogwheel king, she my lovely queen!
With a happiness greater than the world has ever seen,
It wouldn't even have mattered if I wasn't worth a bean.

But I can never be disloyal to my wife,
I'm a widower now but Georgiana's still my life,
I never thought love could endure beyond the grave,
But it does, and all my feelings for my wife I must save.

Now I must always hide behind a cloak of silent calm
Live the rest of my life without love's soothing balm
Dream of Georgiana, still loving her so

And never letting anybody know,
No, never letting anybody know.

As Babbage comes to the end of his song, there is a violent knocking on the door of the room. Babbage rushes to the door, and a weeping Ada stumbles in, supporting Georgie, who has collapsed but is still conscious.

BABBAGE: Ada, what's the matter?

ADA: Charles, Georgie's ill! We'd only gone a short way towards Manchester Square when she gave a sudden cry and collapsed. Fortunately we were arm-in-arm and I was able to stop her from hitting her head on the pavement. Charles, what can be wrong with her?

BABBAGE: I can't imagine. She's been perfectly well.

He helps Ada carry Georgie to the sofa and they lay her carefully there and Ada gently puts a pillow under Georgie's head.

ADA: Oh, God, what are we to do?

There on the sofa, Georgie DIES.

The lights fade quickly into complete darkness.

When the lights come up again, we see that Babbage and Ada, their heads bowed, are standing looking at Georgie's prostrate form on the sofa, their backs to the audience. Georgie now has a white cloth over her face. Two medical assistants stand close by her.

Ada and Babbage are both deep in grief.

BABBAGE: This is too much for me to bear. First, my wife, now my daughter!

ADA: I know. Oh, Charles, the human body is too much of a mystery. As with all branches of science, there is just too much that isn't known about the body. Medical science today can do almost nothing for anyone. Even if I had got Georgie to a doctor in time, I doubt she could have been saved.

(beat)

I cannot believe that my poor darling friend Georgie is dead. I shall never get over it.

BABBAGE: Neither shall I. I shall go abroad. I can't bear remembering my darling daughter laughing and playing here, in this very room! Oh Georgie! How could a merciful God have decreed you should die so young?

ADA: Maybe God is not always merciful.

BABBAGE: Perhaps not. I have written of miracles and how there is no logical reason why they should not happen. I wish a miracle would happen now, and that Georgie would be brought back to life.

ADA: I wish it too.

BABBAGE: It's very late. You can stay here. The guest room upstairs is tidy. I shall have my butler bring you sheets, blankets and pillows.

ADA: No, thank you, I'd rather sleep here, in this room where Georgie and I have had had such wonderful times.

BABBAGE: Of course. I understand. My butler shall bring the necessary items so you can be completely comfortable here…
Well, goodnight.

ADA: Goodnight, Charles.

She runs up to him and kisses him briefly on the lips, then puts her arms around him and holds him. Finally Babbage gently breaks the embrace and exits. Ada falls asleep on the sofa.

It is now the morning. Ada stretches and yawns. She sees that on the table by the sofa there is a note. She picks it up.

ADA: That's strange. A note from Charles.

(reading it aloud) *My dear Ada, I shall be up early in the morning to make the arrangements for poor Georgie's funeral. Ada, there is something I need to tell you. Yesterday morning, Georgie informed me that some years ago, when you were in Kent, you knew a boy called Tom. I think it is possible I know him too. Whitworth's engineering firm makes some of the parts for my Engines, and a bright young fellow at Whitworth's called Tom Newton, whom I gather comes from a village in Kent, has recently started working on my components. He may be the Tom you know, but I have not told him I know you. I do have his address as sometimes my butler delivers design instructions to him there. Here it is:*

(Ada clasps the note to herself) Oh Tom!... Oh Tom, can it be you? If only Georgie were still alive and could meet you!

SCENE 3 - TOM'S SPARSELY FURNISHED BACHELOR ROOMS

The same day. The evening. The room contains a single bed and a desk and chair, at which Tom is sitting wearing just a shirt and trousers, working on some engineering drawings.

There is a knock on a door to the room. Tom gets up and opens the door.

ADA: Hello, Tom.

TOM: I can't believe my eyes!

ADA: Neither can I. May I come in? That is, if you don't have company.

TOM: No… no, I'm alone here. Please… Ada, you're very welcome.

Ada steps confidently into the room.

TOM: How… how did you find my address?

ADA: I am friends with Mr Babbage, and was friends with his daughter Georgie too. She… she died yesterday. Mr Babbage gave me your address. He knew from Georgie that I often talk about you.

TOM: I'm so sorry to hear about your friend's death.

ADA: You never answered my letters! How could you have done that to me? You told me you loved me.

TOM: But I do love you! And I did reply to your letters! All of them, even the one you wrote asking me why I never replied to your letters! Oh Ada, my letters to you were so full of love, and so were yours to me!

ADA: Why didn't you come to find me?

TOM: I did, but you weren't in and when your butler brought Lady Byron to the door and I'd told her who I was, she said that if ever I came to the house again she would call the local constable and have me taken to gaol!

ADA: I'd never have married William if I'd known you still cared for me! Oh Tom, I didn't receive any of your letters. My mother must have concealed them from me… I did wonder if she might have done, but I couldn't believe even she would do such a thing. How wrong I was! But how… how did you get to be working in London?

TOM: I was done with smithying. The most I could expect was to be a blacksmith one day and live all my life in the same village, and very likely never again see a lady like you, or know anything of the world beyond the village. So I made plans to come to London to seek my fortune. I was lucky. I found a job at Whitworth's engineering works last year. Mr Whitworth thinks highly of me and so does Mr Babbage.

ADA: I'm not surprised.

TOM: I've been working in London for just over a year. As soon as I found work I went back to the village and brought my mother here. She was so happy, living with me in London! She lived here with me, but alas, two months ago she died after being struck by a horse and carriage.

ADA: Oh, Tom, I'm so sorry to hear that. You and I have had so much tragedy in our lives.

TOM: I told Mother all about you and how much I love you and how you and I shared the dream of inventing wonderful things that would change the world. Mother was as sorry as I was when you didn't reply to my letters.

ADA: Oh, Tom. My own mother has ruined everything for us! But it is as I say. I would never have got married if I'd thought you still cared for me.

TOM: Ada... I was in the church at the back when you married Lord King. I didn't let you see me. I'd read about the forthcoming marriage in the *London Gazette*. I couldn't keep away.

(sung dialogue)

But... what difference would it have made, really, if I'd made myself know to you?
You're a lady, the daughter of one of the richest women in England.
I could never have married you, even if you'd known I still care for you.
A lady like you marrying a man from Whitworths? I don't think so.
What a fool I was to love you!

ADA: Tom, there's nothing foolish about love.

(beat)

Is there anyone in your own life?

TOM: No, I just work hard, that's all.
No other woman has ever compared with you, anyway.

ADA: I'm sure you'll meet someone wonderful soon. One day you'll be married too.

TOM: Oh, Ada.

ADA: Oh, Tom.

(spoken)

My husband William spends much of his time at our country estate in Ockham in Surrey, but I am often in London. I can visit you. We can be friends, only friends, but... we can know each other again! It will be wonderful! And you can write to me.

TOM: At what address?

ADA: You can write to me care of my mother at 12 St James's Square.

TOM: *(with deep irony)* Oh yes, what an excellent idea!

ADA: Tom, I assure you that you can write to me at my mother's.

TOM: But how do you know she won't intercept my letters again?

ADA: Because of what I'm going to tell her when I see her shortly. I'm going to St James's Square now to see her.

ADA: I can't say how wonderful it is to see you again!

SONG - FOREVER LOVING FRIENDS

[This melody is based on the song *'Freunderl, mach' dir nicht draus'* from *The Land of Smiles*.]

ADA AND TOM

ADA
I'm going to love being your friend, dear Tom
And there's absolutely nothing wrong
With us caring about each other as friends!
Yes it's clear that we can see
Our romance can not now be
But I love you as my dearest friend!

TOM
Being friends is better than nothing Ada
And no there's nothing wrong
With us caring about each other as friends!
Yes it's clear that we can see
Our romance is not to be
But I love you as my dearest friend!

ADA
Darling, let's never be sad
Or think this lovely friendship's bad
Whatever fate shall for us decree
You'll always have a loving friend in me.
And I think God up high above
Knows friendship generally lasts longer than love,
So let's stay forever loving friends!
Though our hearts by law can't bind
Our friendship really will be divine.

TOM
Darling, I won't be sad
Or think this lovely friendship's bad
It's hard, but yes, I agree
You'll always have a loving friend in me.
And if God really does exist
He will bless this friendly kiss.
(Tom kisses Ada's hand)
So yes, this is wonderful and always will be
And we'll be forever loving friends!

ADA AND TOM
Yes, we'll be forever loving friends!

Ada, her eyes on Tom all the time, waves goodbye then exits.

SCENE 4 - THE STUDY IN LADY BYRON'S LONDON HOME

About an hour later, that same evening. Lady Byron is writing some letters at her desk when Ada enters the room.

ADA: Mother, I've met Tom again.

LADY BYRON: Tom who?

ADA: Tom Newton. The boy I knew when I was in Kent.

LADY BYRON: That ruffian! What's he doing in London?… Did you summon him?

ADA: No, he works for Whitworth's, an engineering firm whose services Mr Babbage uses. Mr Babbage mentioned Tom to me.

LADY BYRON: I might have known Babbage would be involved here somewhere.

ADA: He was only trying to help me. And, as I've told you many times, Tom's not a ruffian. He's no longer a blacksmith's apprentice, either, but is making his way at Whitworth's.

LADY BYRON: I see. And you were no doubt delighted to meet him again.

ADA: Yes, I was.

(beat)

Mama, he answered my letters, but I never received them. You must have concealed them from me!

LADY BYRON: I certainly did. The presumptuous things he wrote! I burnt last letter. To think of a blacksmith's apprentice, corresponding with his betters!

ADA: And I suppose that is why you turned the poor darling boy away when he came to our door to try to talk to me?

LADY BYRON: Yes, Ada, it was.

ADA: Mama, it is only a complete accident of birth that you were born to the wealthy Milbanke family in the county of Durham. A different accident of birth might have made you the wife of a miner, a woman who would have to struggle every day as millions of impoverished people struggle every day. I don't like to say this to my own mother, but you are a wicked woman! I can hardly believe you could do such a terrible unscrupulous thing! Tom thought I never cared for him. If I hadn't met him again, he'd have probably gone to his grave believing that! As for *his* own mother, she did go to her grave believing me to be flighty, haughty and callous!

(sung dialogue)

ADA: You read his letters and burnt them! I can't believe it!
There are no 'betters' in the world, find that truth in the fire and retrieve it!
The poor are people who think and feel and hope just as we do
Except they have to spend most of their lives struggling to make do!

LADY BYRON: I see Tom has been talking to you.

ADA: No! I've worked this out for myself.

(beat)

Now listen to me, Mama. Listen very carefully
If you still wish me to be your daughter, listen well.
I've told Tom, whom I love, that he may write to me here. I've made that quite clear,
On my love for him you'll cast no further evil spell!

LADY BYRON: You speak of your love for him! You are a married woman! What a disgrace!

ADA: Disgrace shall be a mere bagatelle compared to the scandal we'd face
If you conceal Tom's letters from me once more!
If you interfere with his letters again,

If you do, I swear I shall leave William and run away with Tom!
There would be a great scandal, even greater than the one there was
between you and Papa!
Yes much greater than that by far!
I do not wish to leave William. He is a good man
He's been good to me. I don't want to break his heart.
But if you do conceal Tom's letters from me, or open them
I shall carry out my threat.
I wouldn't starve; Tom is making his way in the world.
Now, is this perfectly clear?

LADY BYRON: I suppose so. I am going out.
I think you are the most muddle-headed, silly and disobedient of daughters!
I think you and your father are cursed!

ADA: Well, perhaps, but I could be a lot worse.

LADY BYRON: What do you mean?

ADA: I could be like you!

Lady Byron exits in silent fury.

Ada breaks down and starts weeping.

ADA: Georgie dead! And Tom loves me! And I'm married now and can
never marry him! Can life get any worse than this?

She goes to the sofa and lies down, still weeping, then gradually cries herself to sleep.

   LORD BYRON'S GHOST enters and sings to Ada while she sleeps.

SONG - THE LULLABY

LORD BYRON'S GHOST

Ada, darling daughter, as you sleep alone tonight,
Dreaming of poor Georgie - and how her soul took flight,
Take comfort from this knowledge and please stop being sad -
This afternoon she had a bite of manna with your dad.

I walk across the mystic line that shadows life and death
And all of history I breathe in one time-travelling breath,
Don't fear the silence after life, for there is more, more to come,
You'll start another lifetime, just as you're going numb.

We'll leap six years, my sweet, to eighteen forty-two
You're a mum now, love, but maths is what you really want to do,
And Babbage? You're great friends, but you're pretty certain now
That when it comes to being diplomatic he's no notion how.

To make an Analytical Engine, he needs about thirty grand
And he's been lobbying Whitehall with an embarrassing open hand,
He don't care if they like him, what he wants is public gold
And he needs this very much so desperation makes him bold.

Babbage's latest tactic is to demand an interview
With the minister who's prime – the PM to me and you.
Babbage has a dream to engineer a deal
With that frosty Tory stalwart, good Sir Robert Peel.

I walk across the mystic line that shadows life and death
And all of history I breathe in one time-travelling breath
Don't fear the silence after life, for there is more, so much more to come,
You'll start another lifetime, just as you're going numb.

Lord Byron's Ghost exits.

SCENE 5 - SIR ROBERT PEEL'S OFFICE. FRIDAY NOVEMBER 11 1842. SHORTLY BEFORE 11 AM

Bob Peel, now ROBERT PEEL the Prime Minister, sits at his desk glancing over some papers and using an abacus. He is already on edge at the prospect of a meeting with Babbage. There is a knock at the door of Peel's office.

PEEL: Come in!

Peel's private secretary, SIMMONDS, enters the room.

SIMMONDS: Prime Minister, Mr Babbage and Lady Lovelace are waiting in the anteroom.

PEEL: Lady Lovelace too? I thought I was only going to have Babbage inflicted on me?

SIMMONDS: Prime Minister, you may recall that last week you received a letter from Mr Babbage mentioning that Lady Lovelace would be accompanying him.

PEEL: Did I? I've received so many letters over the past few months from Babbage - mostly asking me to waste public funds on his ridiculous cogwheel contraptions. What must I do to be rid of Babbage and his calculating engines?

SIMMONDS: I'm afraid I don't know, sir.

PEEL: In my opinion, every penny spent on them now is merely throwing good money after bad. Still, I must meet my two guests, I suppose. Would you please summon them?

SIMMONDS: Of course, sir.

Simmonds leaves the room. Peel returns to his work.

There is a knock on the office door. Peel slips the abacus away into the top drawer of his desk just before Babbage strides hastily into Peel's office ahead of Simmonds. Ada, more polite and restrained, comes in third. Simmonds puts on a final spurt, and edges ahead of Babbage.

SIMMONDS: Prime Minister, here are Mr Babbage and Lady Lovelace.

Peel stands up, gives Ada a little bow and shakes her hand.

PEEL: Haven't I seen you before somewhere, Lady Lovelace?

ADA: No, I don't think so.

PEEL: Oh, then I must be mistaken. I am honoured to meet you, Lady Lovelace. I've met your mother, Lady Byron, but have never had the pleasure of meeting you before.

ADA: The pleasure is mine, Sir Robert.

PEEL: *(to Babbage)* We've met briefly before, I think, at Dickens's garden-party last summer.

BABBAGE: Yes, indeed, Sir Robert.

PEEL: *(to Ada and Babbage)* Sit down please.

Ada and Babbage sit down on chairs near Peel's desk. Peel goes to sit down at the chair behind his desk.

PEEL: Can I offer either of you a cup of Mr Harrod's tea or coffee?

BABBAGE: Nothing for me, thank you, Sir Robert.

ADA: Nor for me, thank you.

PEEL: *(glancing at Simmonds)* That will be all, Simmonds.

SIMMONDS: Very well, sir.

Simmonds exits.

PEEL: So, Babbage, how is your Differential Engine coming along?

BABBAGE: I think you mean the Difference Engine.

PEEL: Yes, of course. My apologies.

ADA: Its progress has been rather slow, I am afraid.

PEEL: Oh, why is that?

ADA: Primarily due to lack of funds, Sir Robert.

(sung dialogue)

PEEL: But the Government of more than a decade ago voted you more than seventeen thousand pounds!
You promised the Government this Difference Engine.
Yet no Difference Engine has been delivered.

ADA: Sir Robert, the money the Government granted Mr Babbage was generous, but woefully insufficient.

BABBAGE: Sir, I've spent four or five thousand pounds of my own money on the machine
And yet many people say I've used some of the Government's money myself, it's obscene!
These accusations persist and are all great trials
Yes they continue despite my denials.

PEEL: You are too sensitive to that kind of attack!
Just ignore them, don't waste time answering back!
Now as I understand things, you wish for a new Government grant?

ADA: Yes, he does, that's right.

PEEL: But Babbage, why have you never completed a Difference Engine?

BABBAGE: Because while I was still working on it I devised
A machine so ingenious it took even me by surprise,
It's called the Analytical Engine.

PEEL: That may well be
But Babbage, don't you see?
How can you expect a *fresh* five-figure grant?
Allow this, with no Difference Engine completed? I simply can't.

BABBAGE: I've never said I shan't finish the Difference Engine.
But that machine's only capable of applications in one limited part of mathematics; The Analytical Engine, on the other hand, allows all kinds of calculations to be made.

PEEL: So by your own admission you've made the Difference Engine no use whatsoever
By embarking unilaterally on a new cogwheel endeavour!
A second machine, which you haven't completed either!
If you're asking me which of your projects I'd support, I must answer: neither!

ADA: *(to Peel)* What if the Difference Engine were completed and brought into full working operation?

PEEL: If that were to happen, I would certainly be prepared to reconsider this application.

BABBAGE: Sir Robert, it would be absurd folly for me build a
Difference Engine
Before the far more adept and versatile Analytical Engine is completed!

PEEL: That being so, Babbage, I am obliged to have to say
No to your request. Please, complete your Difference Engine without delay!

ADA: Sir Robert, Mr Babbage works on the borders of science and art. I believe that in future scientific history, this interview will play a prominent part!

PEEL: I'm flattered you think so, Lady Lovelace. But my answer to this request for funds must still be no.

SONG - MY MIND IS FULLY OPEN TO YOUR LUDICROUS INVENTION

[Melody and metre inspired by 'My eyes are fully open to my awful situation' from Ruddigore by W.S. Gilbert.]

PEEL, BABBAGE AND ADA.

PEEL

My mind is fully open to your ludicrous invention
I shall go at once to Parliament and tell them your intention
Is to spend your life on hopeless metrical frivolity
And expect the Chancellor to pay for all your silly jollity.
I have a reputation which is worth more than a cabbage
And I'll not be made a fool by you, you verbose fraudster Babbage,
But right now I haven't time for this inconsequential chatter
Besides, it's eighteen forty-two and so it really doesn't matter!

BABBAGE: But I really think it matters.

ADA: Yes, I really think it matters.

PEEL: No, it really doesn't matter.

Singing all at once, BABBAGE, PEEL and ADA repeat their previous lines and each end with 'matter, matter, matter, matter, matter!' while the two who aren't singing the next verse sing 'matter, matter, matter' sub voce until the next verse starts.

BABBAGE

It's true I like to analyse and dissect plain reality
And probe the inner secret of mechanical actuality,
Though let it not be said that I'm a man devoid of human heart,
For when Ada kisses Will it makes my tender senses throb and smart.
But since I am condemned to be a lonely lovelorn stay-at-home

And my dreams of love in seven hues seem fated to be monochrome,
I'll devote this earthly life to engineer my cogwheels' clatter
And in nineteen ninety-two my work will truly matter!

PEEL: No, it'll never really matter.

BABBAGE: But I do think it'll matter.

ADA: Yes, I do think it'll matter.

*Singing all at once, BABBAGE, PEEL and ADA repeat their previous lines
and each end with 'matter, matter, matter, matter, matter!' and the two who
aren't singing the next verse sing 'matter, matter, matter' sub voce until the
next verse starts.*

ADA
If you weren't both so stubborn and so hopelessly old-fashioned
You'd empathise with how the Engines make me feel impassioned!
And if both of you could only be a hundred times astuter,
You would, like me, understand a new meaning of 'computer'!
But since you're both so trapped in your view of male superiority
And are so completely blind to intelligent sorority,
Continue (if you like) to think I'm a crackpot lady hatter...
And now for all futurity this interview will matter!

PEEL: I don't think it'll ever matter.

BABBAGE: But I do think it will matter.

ADA :   I'm *quite certain* it'll matter.

PEEL, BABBAGE, ADA

(very fast)

Continue (if you like) to think her/me a crackpot lady hatter...
And now for all futurity this interview will matter!

Singing all at once, BABBAGE, PEEL and ADA repeat their previous two lines and each end with 'matter, matter, matter, matter, matter!', rising in a crescendo to the end of the song.

SCENE 6 - THE LIVING-ROOM OF TOM NEWTON'S HOUSE IN KENSINGTON

A few hours later. Tom, in his shirt-sleeves, is working at papers at his desk. There are some sharp knocks on the door. Tom gets up and goes to the door. A tearful Ada hurries into his room.

ADA: I simply had to come.

TOM: How did the interview with Peel go?

ADA: It was a complete disaster! I want to take my mind off it. Tell me, how are things at Whitworth's?

TOM: Ada, I've not had a chance to write; everything's been so busy over the past week. I'm not at Whitworth's any more.

ADA: Oh, no! Not another calamity? What happened?

TOM: Ada dear, it's good news, not bad! I've gone into business for myself, along with three men from Whitworth's who were in my department.

ADA: How was Mr Whitworth about that?

TOM: Perfectly happy. Indeed, it was he who suggested that I take the three men with me to help me. He said 'I don't want to lose you, Newton, but you've a big future ahead of you and I won't stand in your way. I'll even be your first customer!'

ADA: Really? He said that?

TOM: Yes! He's given me a contract to make a particular kind of camshaft for him that needs to be machined to a very precise tolerance. So now I'm the owner of Thomas Newton Engineering Limited. But never mind about me. What's wrong?

ADA: Oh, Tom, the meeting with Peel was so awful! It went just as you feared it would: Charles was cantankerous and disrespectful and instead of seeking to appeal to Peel's business instincts, which I think might possibly have worked, Charles just started complaining about how he was seen by the public.

TOM: I knew Babbage would do that. He's a brilliant man, but he's got no restraint, no restraint at all, and no idea about how to be diplomatic. So Peel said no?

ADA: Yes. Oh, Tom, I'm so sad about how the meeting with Peel turned out. Please tell me something happy!

TOM: Very well, I shall, Ada, I'm engaged to be married!

ADA: You are?

TOM: Yes! Her name is Florence and she's a fine woman. There was never anyone else for me but you… but…

ADA: I know. Fate intruded into our lives. But you and I have a wonderful friendship. I really really hope you and Florence will both be very happy.

TOM: Thank you so much. Ada, I've an idea for you. As Babbage appears pretty much to have ruined his chances with the government, why don't you write an article about the Analytical Engine for a scientific journal, and get it published, and try to win support for Babbage's ideas that way?

ADA: That's excellent! I'd never have thought of that. I'll do it!

TOM: I've heard that the journal *Scientific Memoirs* is looking for new and interesting contributions.

ADA: You're so kind … Darling Tom, there's something else I need to tell you. I haven't been well.

TOM: What's wrong?

ADA: Nothing serious, I hope. A woman's complaint. I'm only mentioning it because... well, because I tell you everything. I haven't told William yet. He worries so. I'm sure I'll be fine, but... well, we'll see.

TOM: What does your doctor say?

ADA: I haven't told him either. What's the point? Please don't worry about me: I'm sure I'll be fine. I must dash. I'll see you soon. And yes, I'll write an article about the Analytical Engine!

Tom and Ada embrace, then Ada exits.

SCENE 7 - ADA'S STUDY IN HER COUNTRY HOME IN OCKHAM, SURREY, SHE SHARES WITH WILLIAM AND HER CHILDREN

Ada is working hard at her desk on the article. BYRON and ANNABELLA, two of Ada's three children, are standing close by her, in their pyjamas.

BYRON: What work are you doing, Mama?

ADA: An article about the Analytical Engine and the Difference Engine.

BYRON: Did they have a fight?

ADA: No, darling, they're the two inventions of Mr Babbage, that kindly and friendly gentleman who often comes to dinner.

ANNABELLA: Byron calls him Mr Cabbage.

ADA: I shouldn't worry. The Prime Minister says much worse things about him, I'm sure. Well, goodnight darlings, I need to get on with my work.

BYRON: Goodnight, Mama. I still think they should have a fight.

ANNABELLA: So do I!

Byron and Annabella exit.

ADA: *(to herself)* I envy my darling children, that they can go to bed. I'm so tired, but I need to keep working..
(she stretches and yawns) I think I'll have a little nap, after all, then I can get back to writing my article.

Ada lays her head down on her desk and falls asleep.

While she sleeps, she dreams of Babbage's machines having a fight.

THE ANALYTICAL ENGINE and THE DIFFERENCE ENGINE come onstage. They hate and despise each other.

SONG - OH, I'M POSITIVELY ANALYTICAL

THE ANALYTICAL ENGINE AND THE DIFFERENCE ENGINE

ANALYTICAL ENGINE
Oh, I'm positively analytical,
Completely geopolitical,
Mechanically mission-critical,
Don't you wish you were an Engine like me?

DIFFERENCE ENGINE
No! I just think you're arthritical
Totally sybaritical,
Bossy and hypercritical,
I don't want to be in any way like thee!

ANALYTICAL ENGINE
Your silly rhyming responses bore me,
Don't you realise Ada adores me?
She thinks I'm even better than the Jacquard loom,
And when I'm fully built I'll fill a room!

DIFFERENCE ENGINE
If Ada had been older than six years old when I was born,
She would surely have told you: you're brimful of corn!
At least I'm one-seventh built, you're just a plan
On the drawing-board of a very eccentric man!

ANALYTICAL ENGINE
Only an idiot would malign his inventor,
I wish I could tell Babbage you're a dissenter
And that it really was a dreadful shame
He devised a basic cogwheel brain!

DIFFERENCE ENGINE: You arrogant twit!

ANALYTICAL ENGINE: You're full of... tripe!

DIFFERENCE ENGINE: Just give it a rest!

ANALYTICAL ENGINE: I'm simply the best!

DIFFERENCE ENGINE: You need a good oil!

ANALYTICAL ENGINE: You're a cogwheel boil!

DIFFERENCE ENGINE: You're a social pariah!

ANALYTICAL ENGINE: Go melt in the fire!

ANALYTICAL ENGINE AND DIFFERENCE ENGINE
Babbage and Ada know I'm the best
You're simply a waste of cogs,
You're a pointless waste of space
And mad as a box of frogs!

When Babbage wakes up in the morning
You're the one he ought to dismantle,
And I for one will bless the day
That you are totally cancelled!

ANALYTICAL ENGINE
I'm the king of all cogwheel aces,
That you can never deny;
I can work out to twenty-five places
An accurate value for pi!

DIFFERENCE ENGINE
Maybe… but I'll be completed
By the Science Museum's crew
And I'll be treated like a miracle –
A *bona fide* metal miracle –
In the year of our Lord, ninety-two!

They exit as Ada wakes up.

ADA: What a terrible dream! I wonder what it meant by 'ninety-two'. 1892? Does that mean the Difference Engine will be built when I'm an old lady? If so, will the Analytical Engine be built then too?

(beat)

Well, I'd better go and splash some cold water on my face then get back to work. There's a lot to do.

SCENE 8 - BABBAGE'S STUDY AT HIS HOME ON DORSET STREET

Three months later. Ada watches Babbage finish reading her work.

BABBAGE: You've worked very hard on this article, Ada, I can see that.

ADA: Yes, I spent more than three months on it.

BABBAGE: And what you've written is certainly interesting.

ADA: *(encouraged)* Charles, I've sometimes wondered if even you do not fully understand the consequences of the machines you've invented, especially the Analytical Engine.

BABBAGE: What on earth do you mean?

ADA: It is all there in what I've written.

BABBAGE: Yes, I can see that.

ADA: So… what do you think?

(sung dialogue)

BABBAGE: Well, there's much good and excellent material here
But also much that in my opinion needs to be deleted

ADA: Such as what?

BABBAGE: Your enthusiasm for the Engines project is clear,
But I think by the scale of the writing challenge you've been defeated!

ADA: What are you talking about?

BABBAGE: Ada, I concern myself above all with facts,
Science is invariably provable, and must be totally exact!
Much of what you've written here seems rather
To be the kind of woolly thinking I'd expect from your father!

ADA: Don't bring Papa into it!

BABBAGE: I've really no choice!
You and Lord Byron seem to speak here with one voice!
Ada, your article is full of idiosyncratic glosses
Which, if I were your teacher, would receive a row of crosses!

(spoken)

ADA: Such as?

BABBAGE: Well, here for example.

(he turns the pages and now quotes Ada's writing)

'We may say most aptly, that the Analytical Engine weaves algebraical patterns just as the Jacquard loom weaves flowers and leaves.'

What a strange thing to say!

ADA: What's strange about it? You agreed that a Jacquard loom could be a kind of computer, a machine rather than a clerk.

BABBAGE: Yes, I did, but only in a theoretical sense. I see no connection at all between the loom of Monsieur Jacquard and my Analytical Engine, other than that of course I borrowed Jacquard's notion of using punched cards, which I have always freely admitted.

ADA: But Charles, I believe that one day, Analytical Engines shall be used precisely for that purpose, for a kaleidoscope of applications, not only to carry out calculations! I also have invented my own algorithm: the algorithm of the Analytical Engine. It's all set down there, in the article. My algorithm could indeed be used to give the Analytical Engine a myriad of wonderful practical and useful applications!

BABBAGE: Oh Ada, that could never be! Sometimes your mind is completely befuddled! The Analytical Engine is designed to carry out mechanical calculations, that's all! Your entire article is full of the thinking I find so inexplicable, woefully speculative and impractical.

ADA: I don't agree. Why should not science be poetical as well as mechanical?

BABBAGE: How can science possibly be *poetical?*

ADA: I believe it needs to be poetical if we are to extract from science all it can possibly give us. Now, I have something else to say as well.

(she pauses, she knows this is her big moment)

I really have something of great importance to ask you, Charles, and I hope you
give what I suggest deep and serious consideration. Please, for your own sake, don't lightly reject what I say.

(beat)

Charles, I propose that you focus your intellect, your remarkable and inventive scientific genius, on the actual *building* of the machines and on working with
the workmen and craftsmen who assist you in that bid. I propose you delegate to me the responsibility of winning people over to the engines.

Babbage looks thoughtful but stays silent for a few moments. Ada looks hopeful and optimistic.

ADA: Well, what's your answer?

BABBAGE: I am sorry to have to tell you, Ada, but I shall never, under any circumstances, do this.

ADA: Charles, please...

BABBAGE: No, Ada, let me speak. You've had your say. You forget yourself. I am the instigator of the engines and their inventor, and it can only be me who takes responsibility for relations between the engines and the people who need to be influenced in favour of them.

ADA: But you shall fail with others just as you failed with Peel!

BABBAGE: But then I shall own the failures just as I own the successes!

ADA: What nonsense! Why should you want to own any failures? And besides, there haven't been any successes. The Analytical Engine is nothing more than plans, not a working machine. I believe I can help transform it into reality! Agree to what I suggest, Charles. Agree to it, I beg you! You'll never conjure the support you need for your engines if you insist on working alone!

BABBAGE: Perhaps not. But I am the master of the Difference Engine and the Analytical Engine and they shall succeed or fail by my own efforts.

ADA: And if you do fail? Then the whole of humankind shall be deprived forever of the benefits of the Analytical Engine! If you refuse what I offer you shall fail. For you cannot do everything yourself and hope to be successful. Surely more than twenty years of trying to win support for your engines has convinced you of that?

BABBAGE: I still say no!

ADA: And I say you are an utterly obstinate man! You know I've never truly desired anything but to help you turn your plans for the engines into reality! That is my one remaining dream!

BABBAGE: It is my dream, not yours!

ADA: No, it is mine too! It has been my dream ever since I met you almost a decade ago! When I was a girl I dreamed of flying, but that dream was stolen from me by my mother. She pretended she stopped me trying to fly because she was concerned for my safety. But the truth is that she hates me having any dreams at all. My new dream was to help you bring cogwheel computation into the world, and you - who are my friend - want to rob me of that too. Oh Charles, for the sake of all that's good, please say yes to my suggestion that I help you! I am sure you saying yes would be for the good of the Engines and for your own benefit too!

(beat)

The truth is, I haven't been feeling at all well of late, and your saying yes to my suggestion would bring me a new determination and a new focus for my energies.

BABBAGE: Ada, I am truly sorry you have not been feeling well. But

I must speak very plainly. Nobody shall ever supplant me as the master of the Engines, and especially not a woman! Now, I need to go and do some work.

Ada shrieks with dismay. Babbage stomps out of the room. Ada courageously just stands there, recovering her spirits, then breaks into song:

SONG - AS A WOMAN I WAS DOOMED FROM THE START

ADA

I fell in love with the Analytical Engine,
It held the key to beauty and absolute truth,
I dreamed it would unlock the vision that gripped me,
The wonders I had harboured since my youth;

The wonders I had harboured since my youth.
If only Charles had accepted my vision
Only Tom saw what I could see:
The wonders of technology now denied me,
My algorithm still fills this ailing heart,
But as a woman I was doomed from the start,
As a woman I was doomed from the start.

After Ada finishes her song, she walks off in sorrow.

SCENE 9 - LADY BYRON'S DRAWING-ROOM

Saturday November 27 1852. Nine years later.

Ada is on her deathbed. Lady Byron is with her.

LADY BYRON: I sometimes wonder why you remained friends with Babbage after he rejected your very sensible offer nine years ago.

ADA: I know. But somehow, despite everything, I know he needs me. And I need him. Perhaps that is because we are both failures.

LADY BYRON: You have been a good mother, and a good wife, and in some… no, many respects a good daughter. There is nothing of failure in that. I know you have suffered much, Ada. But suffering cleanses the soul and readies it to meet the Lord… As for Babbage, it doesn't surprise me in the least that he has made no progress at all with his Engines since then. I have no doubt that he never will.

ADA: Please ask William to come to see me here.

LADY BYRON: Certainly not. He was extremely rude to me the last time he came.

ADA: Only because he wants me to be with him, at home in Ockham.

LADY BYRON: Ada, you are dying. It is I, your mother, who is looking after you now. You have already said goodbye to your children, and it was most affecting. You have certainly always been a good mother. As for Babbage, I have given my butler instructions that if he as much as shows his face here, they are to summon the Peelers.

ADA: Oh, the police. An invention of which Sir Robert Peel did approve!

LADY BYRON: He invented them, Ada.

ADA: Yes, I know. I know that only too well.

There is a knock on the door of the room. Lady Byron goes to the door and opens it. Walker is there.

WALKER: Ma'am, there is a visitor.

LADY BYRON: Not Babbage or Lord Lovelace, I hope?

WALKER: No, Ma'am. He says his name is Sir Thomas Newton.

LADY BYRON: Sir Thomas Newton, the famous engineer! Oh my goodness! Well, don't just stand there, Walker! Invite him in! Invite him in!

Walker exits, then returns after a moment with Tom. Walker exits.

TOM: Good afternoon, Lady Byron.

LADY BYRON: *(grovelling pathetically)* Oh, good afternoon, Sir Thomas! What a great honour to be visited by you! So, we meet at last! I'm so sorry about the misunderstanding when you visited all those years ago. I... well, I thought you were someone else. You are the blacksmith's apprentice who has risen to become a great pioneer in the field of engineering precision, and is now a knight of the realm.

TOM: I have been fortunate, Lady Byron.

ADA: Tom is much too modest, Mama. He has worked very hard, and taken great risks, and been vindicated in everything he has done. So you see, mother, you were wrong to call him a 'ruffian'.

LADY BYRON: 'Ruffian'? My dear Ada, I never said any such thing! You misheard me, my dear girl. I must have been speaking too softly and sweetly as usual. What I said was, Thomas must have had a 'rough' path to success.

ADA: Yes, of course, Mama. You also called Tom an 'urchin'.

LADY: I said nothing of the kind, my dear. What I said was, the *church in* the village near Bifrons House was very pretty.

TOM: Ada, I am so sorry I haven't come before. I travelled yesterday all the way to Ockham in Surrey to try to see you, only to be told by Lord Lovelace that you're here. How are you?

ADA: I am in much pain, Tom. My health has been poor for several years, as you know only too well. Thank you so much for your wonderful friendship during those years; it has meant so much to me. The past few weeks have been very difficult for me health-wise. I don't think I am much longer for this world.

(to Lady Byron)

Mother, would you please leave us alone for a little while?

LADY BYRON: By all means.

(grovelling, to Tom)

Thank you for coming, Sir Thomas. I am honoured to meet you at last. I am… very sorry about not showing Ada your letters. I had formed an erroneous opinion of you, and was trying to protect Ada.

TOM: Lady Byron, that all happened a long time ago. But in any case I forgive you.

LADY BYRON: Thank you, Sir Thomas, thank you.

Lady Byron exits in a pathetic, fawning, grovelling manner.

ADA: Tom, Mr Dickens came to read some weeks ago from the chapter in *Dombey and Son* where little Paul Dombey dies. I found it most affecting.

TOM: Yes, I met Dickens at John Forster's dinner-party last week, and Dickens told me he'd read to you. I thanked him from the bottom of my heart for doing so. Ada, in what way has your health got worse recently?

ADA: Read this, Tom. It's a letter which my doctor, Dr West, sent to my mother a few days ago about my condition. My mother has let me see it; she believes that the truth must always be confronted. Read it. Read it to me. Let us face reality.

TOM: Do you really want me to read it?

ADA: Yes.

TOM: *'Lady Lovelace's disease is cancer; the final symptoms of which appeared between eighteen months and two years ago; consisting not in pain but in frequent and alarmingly profuse haemorrhages'*
Cancer! oh no, I can't read this anymore.

Ada puts the letter beneath her pillow again. Tom sits next to her and holds her hands in his.

ADA: Please don't be sad, Tom. Please don't be sad. Life is so wonderful. Even when one completely fails, as I have failed, in all my ambitions, life is still wonderful. Human beings - what an extraordinary mixture of beauty and greatness and accomplishment and folly and self-destructiveness we are!

SONG - I'M LYING HERE SADLY WATCHING THE SKY

ADA

[reprise of SITTING ALONE, LOOKING UP AT THE SKY, same melody and some changes to the lyrics]

I'm lying here sadly watching the sky
Seeing the clouds and my life all fly by
And regretting I didn't make much of a mark on the world
As I yearned to do so much when I was a girl.

I saw the whole world was changing, progress in strides
I thought if men can achieve it, why can't I?
But I see that the whole world has no need of me...

TOM: *(speaking)* Ada, the world has an infinite need of you...

ADA: (speaking) If it did, why did it make me feel that it didn't want what I could offer it?

(singing)

But I see that the whole world has no need of me...
And I'll never be who I wanted to be,
And I've so much pain in this bodily state
That I really will be quite glad to be late.

Yet one day, perhaps, my ideas will find soil
To grow in, and justify my toil...

(she sings now in a more personal, more dreamy kind of way)

Soaring so high, chasing the stars
Thousands of miles won't seem so far
Way down here, I'm just some girl
But one day soon, *(tearfully)* I may change this world…

ADA: *(speaking)* Darling Tom, William is a good man and a fine father to my children, but you've been the true love of my life. Goodbye, Tom.

Ada DIES. An unusual light now shines on her.

Tom freezes into stillness. Lord Byron's Ghost enters, holding GEORGIE'S GHOST by the hand. Lord Byron's Ghost and Georgie's Ghost sit down on the chair next to ADA'S GHOST.

ADA GHOST: *(seeing them)* Papa? Georgie?

LORD BYRON'S GHOST: Yes, darling, it's me. It's good to see you again, beloved sole daughter of my house and heart!

GEORGIE'S GHOST: Oh, Ada! We'll be together now for ever!

Georgie's Ghost enfolds Ada in her arms as the lights fade to darkness.

A few moments later, the lights come up. One by one, all the main characters come on now in turn, speaking (or maybe singing) about their lives. Tom enters first.

TOM:
Dear Ada! Dear darling Ada!
I never forgot her, ever! I died at the age of ninety-seven,
I didn't pass away until May the third, nineteen eleven.
Be assured I always remembered my early penniless years -
I set up in my Will a school for poor but eager engineers.

I missed my beloved Ada so! I thought of her each day
I think an Engine would have come to birth had Ada had her way.
I travelled widely, and in the States, I met Orville and Wilbur Wright,

And watched them both at Kitty Hawk when they made their maiden flight!

(spoken)

As I saw their airplane soar, that first ever flight, all I could think about was Ada. How I wished that she had been there with me!

Tom exits. William enters.

WILLIAM:
I really wasn't quite as dense, as people seem to think
And when my darling Ada died, I didn't turn to drink,
But did my best to be the dad my children really needed
No plea from them would go unheard, no fair request unheeded.

In eighteen sixty-five I married a kindly lady called Jane
She wasn't quite an Ada when it came to having a brain
But Jane made me very happy, and so it came to be
That I died at the age of eighty-eight, in eighteen ninety-three.

William exits. Sir Robert Peel enters.

SIR ROBERT PEEL:
I fully realise that I'm the villain of this story
And I don't anticipate winning much posthumous glory
In the history of computing; still, I helped to keep the peace
By bringing to the world, the first force of... police!

I deserved to live, I think, until late in the century
But fate, that malicious elf, had a different destiny for me,
My pomp and pride that flowed so wide, abruptly stopped their course
And I died in eighteen-fifty, after falling off my horse.

Sir Robert Peel exits. Babbage enters.

BABBAGE:
What a fool I was to say no to my trusting ally Ada!

I should have gratefully agreed… in that wise I betrayed her,
But don't blame me completely, I was born many years ago
When people thought machines and ladies together just caused woe.

My reputation nowadays is really rather strong
And fortunately people tend to forget I did my Ada wrong.
Today, when Ada and I, invisibly, stroll around your time
We're affectionate companions, and our friendship is sublime.

Babbage exits.

LORD BYRON'S GHOST:
What a wonderful daughter she was! How proud I'll always be
That Ada and I now lie side-by-side in the family tomb for eternity!
Dear future dwellers, let me tell you about dear Ada:
Today, in your world, she's seen as a crusader
For understanding, better than Babbage, the potential of the computer,
Today, a billion Ada fans eternally salute her!

*As Lord Byron's Ghost leaves, Ada and Tom, BOTH IN MODERN DRESS,
and played by the same actors, run onto the stage from opposite sides. They are
each carrying a modern digital tool such as an ipad or a smartphone. As they
near each other, they both become shyer and eye each other more cautiously.*

MODERN ADA: Hello.

MODERN TOM: Hello.

MODERN ADA: Haven't I seen you before somewhere?

MODERN TOM: No, I don't believe so.

MODERN ADA: I once had a dream in which you saved me from some
country children who were making fun of me.

MODERN TOM: How weird! I had that dream too.

MODERN ADA: Thank you for rescuing me, anyway even if it was only in a dream.

MODERN TOM: You're welcome.

MODERN ADA: Shall we be Facebook friends?

MODERN TOM: I'd love that.

(looking up at the sky)

Look at that plane up there! I know we take flying for granted nowadays, but it always seems magical to me.

MODERN ADA: And to me.

MODERN TOM: Maybe one day we'll fly off somewhere on holiday!

MODERN ADA: That would be lovely!

Ada and Tom kiss passionately.

SONG - OH, TOM, MY LOVE! (REPRISE)

MODERN ADA AND MODERN TOM

MODERN ADA
>Oh, Tom, my love!
>Now we don't need to part
>And deep romantic art
>Brims in our hearts,
>Oh, Tom, my love!

MODERN TOM
>Oh, Ada, dear!
>Now I'll forever stay here
>And feel delight you're near!
>Our future together is clear,
>Oh, Ada, dear!

MODERN ADA
>Oh, Tom, my love!

MODERN TOM
>Oh, Ada, dear!

MODERN ADA
>Now we don't need to part
>And deep romantic art
>Brims in our hearts,
>Oh, Tom, my love!

MODERN TOM
>Oh, Ada, dear!
>Now I'll forever stay here
>And feel delight you're near!
>Our future together is clear,
>Oh, Ada, dear!

SONG - WE'VE SEEN ALL OUR DREAMS COME TRUE

(sung to the same tune as THE WONDERS OF MACHINERY)

MODERN ADA AND MODERN TOM

MODERN ADA AND MODERN TOM
>We've seen all our dreams come true,
>The wonders of machinery,
>We totally adore our view
>Of technological scenery.
>
>Magic pictures on the wall,
>Documentaries, contemporary dramas,

We'll have a takeaway and watch it all
Comfy together in our pyjamas.

Carriages without a horse,
They're called automobiles of course,
And it's definitely them we hear
And watch together, on *Top Gear.*

MODERN ADA

But none of this matters half as much
As you and I being together,
Now I can feel your lovely touch
In sun, in rain, in every weather.

MODERN TOM

Yes, none of this matters half as much
As you and I being together,
Now I can feel your lovely touch
In sun, in rain, in every weather.

MODERN ADA AND MODERN TOM

Yes, technology's our second dream,
And now we know we love each other
Our love is still as hot as steam…

MODERN TOM *(still singing)*

I just can't wait to meet your mother!

MODERN ADA *(still singing)*

Thank goodness now I've got another!

The actress who played Lady Byron comes on as MODERN ADA'S
MOTHER. She is dressed in a cute, rather sexy outfit, is obviously a
much nicer person now, and hurries to greet Ada and Tom and embraces

them both. Lord Byron's Ghost and Georgie's Ghost emerge from one of the wings, staying close together and they applaud this scene of love and harmony as

THE CURTAIN FALLS

Please note: all enquiries for performance rights for *Ada's Algorithm - the Ada Lovelace musical* should be directed to Francesca Garratt at The Conrad Press

Email: francescagarratt@theconradpress.com